T0246491

THE BASICS OF

CHEMICAL REACTIONS

THE BASICS OF
CHEMICAL
REACTIONS

ANNE O'DALY

Published in 2024 by The Rosen Publishing Group, Inc.
2544 Clinton Street, Buffalo, NY 14224

First edition published 2014. Second edition 2024.

Text and Editor: Lindsey Lowe
Children's Publisher: Anne O'Daly
Design Manager: Keith Davis
Designer: John Woolford
Picture Manager: Sophie Mortimer
Consultant: Adrian Dingle

Cataloging-in-Publication Data

Names: O'Daly, Anne, 1966-.
Title: The basics of chemical reactions / Anne O'Daly.
Description: Second edition. | New York : Rosen Young Adult, 2024. | Series:
  Core concepts | Includes glossary and index.
Identifiers: ISBN 9781499475470 (pbk.) | ISBN 9781499475487 (library bound) |
  ISBN 9781499475494 (ebook)
Subjects: LCSH: Chemical reactions--Juvenile literature. | Chemistry-
  -Juvenile literature.
Classification: LCC QD501.O34 2024 | DDC 541'.39--dc23

Some of the images in this book illustrate individuals who are models.
The depictions do not imply actual situations or events.

Manufactured in the United States of America

CPSIA Compliance Information: Batch #CW24RYA. For further information,
contact Rosen Publishing, New York, New York, at 1-800-237-9932.

Find us on

CONTENTS

CHAPTER 1

What Are Chemical Reactions?

A chemical reaction is a process that changes one set of chemicals into another. Chemical reactions turn food into energy, coal into fire, and iron into rust. They are happening all round us—some inside our bodies.

Without chemical reactions, the world would be a boring place. A chemical reaction is any process that changes one substance into another. Some reactions happen naturally, such as when we digest food or when metal objects become rusty. Other reactions are produced by people to improve their lives, such as burning fuel to power engines or keep homes warm.

Reactions involve the interaction between two basic components of the universe—matter and energy. Scientists call any substance that takes up space "matter." Rocks, water, and air are all made of

↑ All chemical reactions involve energy. Burning, or combustion, is a chemical reaction that releases energy. The energy can be used to provide heat.

CHEMISTRY AT HOME

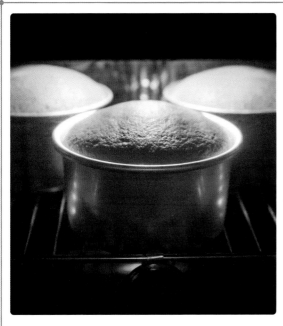

Using chemical reactions, chemists have created countless products we use every day. Plastics are chains of different types of chemicals strung together. Soaps and toothpastes are made from fatty substances using chemical reactions. Recipes tell us how to use chemical reactions to cook food.

← Baking a cake involves chemical reactions. Heat causes baking powder to produce tiny bubbles of gas that make the cake light and fluffy. Sugars and proteins are broken down at high temperatures and rearranged.

matter. Energy is the ability to do work—to move or reshape matter in some way. Heat, light, and electricity are types of energy. During a chemical reaction, energy works to reorganize matter.

Elements

All matter on Earth is made of elements. An element cannot be reduced to a simpler substance by a chemical reaction. All elements are made of atoms. An atom is the smallest piece of an element that still has the properties of that element. However, atoms do have smaller parts, which have other properties. Chemists represent each element with a symbol of one or two letters.

Atoms are often found in simple combinations called molecules. A pure substance consists of only one type of molecule, which is described by a molecular formula. The formula shows how many atoms of each element are involved. One of the simplest molecules is hydrogen (H_2). This formula shows that the molecule contains two hydrogen (H) atoms. The formula for water is H_2O; two hydrogen atoms are connected to one oxygen (O) atom.

Reactants and Products

The substances you start with in a chemical reaction are called the reactants. The new substances that are created are called the products. Chemists write the reactants and products as chemical equations. Numbers are used in the equation to indicate how much of each substance is needed. The arrow indicates that a chemical reaction has taken place and something new has been produced. A chemical reaction can yield one or more products.

A simple chemical reaction occurs when carbon dioxide (CO_2) forms. This molecule contains carbon (C) and oxygen (O) atoms. These elements combine to produce carbon dioxide. The equation looks like this:

$$C + O_2 \rightarrow CO_2$$

A balanced chemical equation shows exactly how much of the reactant and product are involved in the reaction.

KEY DEFINITIONS

Atom: The smallest piece of an element that still retains the properties of that element.
Chemical reaction: A process in which atoms of different elements join together or break apart.
Element: A substance made up of just one type of atom.
Matter: Anything that can be weighed.

Chemists balance equations to determine how many reactants are needed to produce new substances. A balanced equation is one where the number of atoms on one side is the same as the number on the other.

NATURAL GAS

Natural gas is a fuel used in ovens and on cooktops. It releases lots of heat when it burns. The gas is mainly methane, a substance with molecules made of carbon and hydrogen atoms. The burning takes place when methane reacts with oxygen. The products of this reaction are carbon dioxide and water.

⬇ The equation for this reaction (below) is balanced: The number of each type of atom is the same on both sides.

methane	oxygen	carbon dioxide	water	heat
CH_4	$2O_2$	CO_2	$2H_2O$	

What Are Subatomic Particles?

The smaller parts of the atom are the pieces involved in a chemical reaction. These parts are called subatomic particles. At the center of the atom is the nucleus. The nucleus is a densely packed ball of positively charged particles called protons. These are mixed

⬆ The products of chemical reactions are often very different from the reactants. Here, a liquid reactant is reacting. Solid blue cobalt (II) hydroxide precipitate is formed by adding sodium hydroxide to solution containing cobalt (II) ions.

with neutral (noncharged) particles called neutrons. Opposite charges attract, while like charges repel. The positively charged protons in the nucleus attract negatively charged particles called electrons. Electrons are much smaller than protons. They move in clouds around the nucleus. It is the electrons that allow an atom to form bonds with other atoms. How the electrons from two atoms interact determines which type of bond forms. Electrons can be given, taken, or shared to create a bond between two or more atoms. During a chemical reaction, bonds linking some atoms are broken and new bonds are built between others. When atoms of different elements bond, they create a substance called a compound.

Compounds often look very different than the reactants that produced them. For example, sugar is a compound of carbon, hydrogen, and oxygen. Pure hydrogen and oxygen are both invisible gases, and pure carbon forms both diamonds and graphite. Together these elements form many of the compounds called carbohydrates, one of which is sugar.

Energy Behind Reactions

Energy is an essential part in any chemical reaction. It is required to break a chemical bond, and energy is also released when another bond forms. Heat is one type of energy that is often involved in chemical reactions. Some reactions will take in heat. Other chemical reactions will give off heat, such as burning fuel.

THE PERIODIC TABLE OF THE ELEMENTS

Chemists often consult the periodic table, which is one of the most powerful tools used in chemistry. The periodic table is an organized list that provides information about individual elements and groups of elements. The vertical columns in the table are called groups, or families, of elements. Members of each group generally react in the same way.

Each group has a set of known properties. For example, the column on the left of the periodic table is known as the alkali metals. These are very reactive elements, such as sodium and potassium. Instead of memorizing the properties for every element (there are currently 118, with more being discovered all the time), chemists simply consult the periodic table.

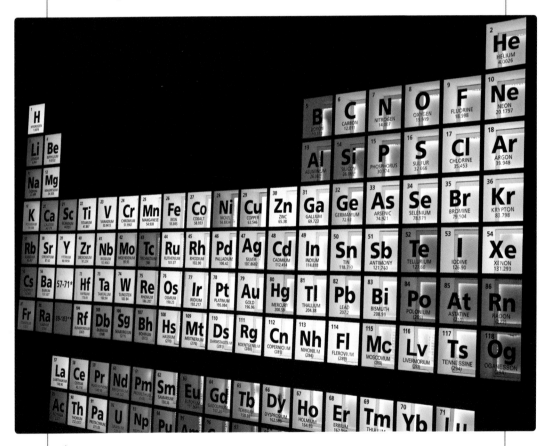

The periodic table of the elements groups together elements with similar properties for easy reference. Chemists consult the periodic table when they need to.

THE CHEMISTRY OF LIFE

Without chemical reactions, life could not exist. Like the bodies of all life-forms, the human body is powered by chemical reactions. You inhale oxygen (O_2) when you take a breath of air. When you eat food, your stomach extracts useful chemicals, such as sugar, from it. Oxygen reacts with the sugars in your body to produce carbon dioxide (CO_2) and water (H_2O). Biologists call this chemical reaction respiration. The reaction releases energy from sugar, which keeps the body alive. You exhale the products of respiration with each breath.

Plants complete the same chemical reaction in reverse—a process called photosynthesis. They take in carbon dioxide and water, and they use the energy in sunlight to produce oxygen and sugar.

← During exercise, the body uses the respiration reaction to release energy from food. The energy is used to power other chemical reactions in the muscles that move the body. Plants also use respiration to release energy, but they also do the opposite through photosynthesis. Photosynthesis takes place in the green parts of plants, mostly in the leaves.

Rearranging the Bonds

When chemical compounds undergo a chemical reaction, energy works to rearrange the bonds between the atoms. For example, consider the equation:

$$AB + C \rightarrow A + BC$$

Elements A and B are bonded to form the AB compound. The AB compound and C element are the reactants. During the reaction, the bond between A and B breaks and a bond between B and C is formed. Element A and the BC compound are the products.

In this reaction, one bond was broken and a new bond between two different atoms was made. The atoms themselves did not change—A did not change to D, for instance. The reaction changed only how the elements were joined.

CHAPTER 2

How Atoms Bond Together

In a chemical reaction, old bonds are broken and new ones form. How a bond between atoms forms depends on the number and position of electrons in an atom's shell.

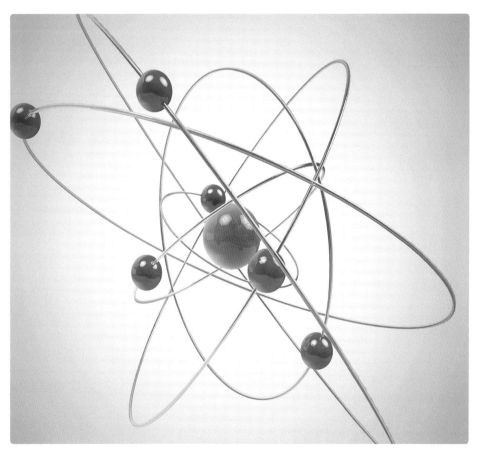

⬆ An atom's nucleus (green in this picture) contains most of its matter. Electrons (blue) move around the nucleus and are the particles that are involved in chemical reactions.

Chemical bonds are created when atoms give, take, or share electrons. There are three types of chemical bonds: ionic, covalent, and metallic. The type of bond formed between atoms depends on how many electrons they have in the atom and how they are arranged.

Electrons

The location of electrons in an atom is one factor that determines how that atom will form bonds. Scientists use two models to explain the location of electrons in the atom—the Bohr model and the quantum mechanics model.

The Bohr model describes electrons orbiting (circling) the nucleus of an atom like the planets orbit the sun. As electrons travel in circles around the nucleus, they are held in place by the pull of the nucleus. The nucleus has a positive charge, which attracts the negative charges of the electrons. This model for the atom works well for very simple atoms, such as hydrogen.

The quantum mechanics model is more mathematical. It describes volumes of space called electron clouds, inside which electrons reside. It is not possible to know exactly where each electron is or how fast it is moving inside a cloud, but their average positions can be calculated. This model is a more accurate way of describing how an atom is put together than the Bohr model.

Energy Levels

In both models, electrons sit at different energy levels. An energy level determines how likely an electron is to be involved in

JOHN DALTON'S ATOMIC THEORY

English chemist John Dalton (1766-1844) is best known for his atomic theory—a basic set of rules explaining how atoms behave, including how they combine with each other. Four of Dalton's rules are still true today:

1) All matter is composed of atoms.
2) All atoms in an element are the same.
3) Atoms combine to form compounds.
4) Atoms are rearranged in a chemical reaction.

A fifth rule, that atoms cannot be divided into smaller particles, was wrong. We now know atoms contain even smaller pieces.

a chemical reaction and form a bond. Electrons in energy levels farthest from the nucleus are most likely to become involved in a reaction because they are held only weakly by the nucleus.

Atoms can have several energy levels. The level closest to the nucleus can only hold two electrons. Chemists call this the lowest energy level. The levels farther from the nucleus can hold more than two electrons. Electrons need more energy to sit in the outer energy levels.

The energy levels are sometimes called orbitals—the areas in which electrons orbit around the nucleus. Chemists also describe them as electron shells because they can be thought of as layers, or shells, surrounding the nucleus.

SOLID, LIQUID, OR GAS

Matter comes in three states—solid, liquid, and gas. Each state depends on the arrangement of the atoms or molecules. Matter changes from one state to another by being heated or cooled. Solids are closely packed groups of atoms or molecules. The atoms and molecules can vibrate back and forth, but they cannot move past one another. When a solid is heated, it melts into a liquid. A liquid is a collection of atoms or molecules that are less closely packed than in a solid. The molecules have enough spaces between them to flow past each other. Heating a liquid causes it to boil into a gas.

A gas is a group of fast-moving atoms or molecules that are completely separate from each other and moving in all directions. A solid has a fixed shape, a liquid takes on the shape of its container, and a gas spreads out and fills all the available space.

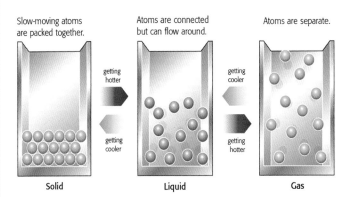

Slow-moving atoms are packed together.

Atoms are connected but can flow around.

Atoms are separate.

getting hotter

getting cooler

getting cooler

getting hotter

Solid

Liquid

Gas

← The state of matter depends on how hot it is. When the atoms are heated, they move more rapidly. This movement begins to break the bonds between them, which results in a change of state.

Number of Electrons

The number of electrons in an atom is the other factor that determines how that atom will react and form bonds. An atom is most stable (unreactive) when its shells are full of electrons. An atom with a full shell will not give, take, or share electrons easily. Because of that, the atom does not get involved in chemical reactions and form bonds.

Electrons fill the inner shells first. The lowest-energy shell has space for just two electrons. Helium atoms have two electrons, and these fill the inner shell. This makes the atom stable. It does not give, take, or share electrons because its shell is full.

Larger atoms have two or more electron shells. The extra shells are larger than the first one and need eight electrons to become stable. Becoming stable with eight electrons is called the octet rule. This rule drives all chemical reactions because atoms will react with each other until they become stable.

KEY TERMS

Metal: A hard but flexible element. Metals are good conductors. Their atoms have only a few outer electrons.
Metalloid: An element that has both metallic and nonmetallic properties.
Nonmetal: An element that is not a metal. Nonmetals are poor conductors. Their atoms tend to have several outer electrons.

Stable atoms are unreactive. Atoms with incomplete outer shells will give, take, or share electrons to fill their energy levels. These atoms are reactive because they take part in chemical reactions. An atom with one electron in its outer shell will give it away easily. Atoms with six or seven outer electrons readily take electrons to fill that shell. When atoms give, take, or share electrons, they create bonds. During a chemical reaction, bonds are broken and built to create new molecules.

Creating Bonds

Atoms have a naturally neutral charge. The positive protons in the nucleus balance out the negative electrons. Because of the location and number of electrons, some atoms create bonds more readily than others. Based on this ability to form bonds, all elements can be divided into three basic types: metals, nonmetals, and metalloids.

Metal atoms have only a few outer electrons and tend to lose them during chemical reactions. Most elements are metals, and they have certain properties.

GROUPS OF ELEMENTS

The number of electrons in the atom's outer shell determines how that element forms bonds and many of its other properties. For this reason, elements are often grouped according to their number of outer electrons. For example, some elements with one outer electron are called alkali metals. Lithium is an alkali metal. It forms bonds by giving away its outer electron. Carbon has four outer electrons and forms bonds by sharing them with other atoms. Fluorine has seven outer electrons, which makes it a member of the halogen group. Halogens bond by taking one electron from another atom. The noble gases have full shells. Argon and helium are noble gases. They do not form bonds at all.

Hydrogen
1 electron
1 outer electron

electron

Helium
2 electrons
2 outer electrons

nucleus

electron shell

Lithium
3 electrons
1 outer electron

Carbon
6 electrons
4 outer electrons

Fluorine
9 electrons
7 outer electrons

Neon
10 electrons
8 outer electrons

WHAT IS THE DIFFERENCE?

When elements combine into a compound, they form a completely new substance that has different properties from the original elements. Compounds are not mixtures of those elements. A mixture contains substances that can be separated from each other easily. A compound can only be separated into its ingredients by a chemical reaction that breaks down its bonds.

← Shown here are samples of pure iron and sulfur. When mixed together (bottom left) and heated, the iron and sulfur atoms react to form the compound iron sulfide (bottom right).

Nearly all metals are solid, shiny, and can conduct electricity. A solid piece of metal contains many free-floating electrons shared among the atoms. These electrons act like stepping stones for an electric charge within the metal, allowing the charge to move within the solid. This property makes metals good materials to use in wires and electric cables.

Nonmetals are the opposite of metals. Nonmetals tend to gain electrons in chemical reactions. They come in all forms and may be liquid, gas, or solid in normal conditions. They are not good at conducting electricity. There are no free-floating electrons to help move an electric charge. Instead, nonmetals are good insulators. Metalloids are semiconductors, which change from being insulators to conductors depending on the conditions.

How strongly an atom holds onto its electrons and pulls electrons away from another atom is called its electronegativity. Nonmetals are more electronegative than metals. Metal atoms have only a few outer electrons, which the atoms give away easily.

What Is an Ionic Bond?

During a chemical reaction, three types of bonds can form: ionic, covalent, or metallic.

↑ Salt is found in desert salt flats and dissolved in seawater.

An ionic bond occurs when a metal atom gives an electron to a nonmetal atom. The atom that gives away an electron loses a negative charge and becomes positively charged itself.

Chemists call atoms that have become charged in this way ions. A positively charged ion is a cation. The atom that takes an electron receives an extra negative charge and becomes a negatively charged ion, or anion. Opposite charges attract each other, so the cation and anion join to form an ionic bond. Bonded ions are called ionic compounds.

A common ionic compound is table salt. Table salt is formed when sodium (Na) bonds with chlorine (Cl). Sodium is a typical metal. It is silvery and conductive, with one electron to give. Chlorine is a nonmetal gas, in need of one electron to complete its octet

KEY TERMS

Conductor: A substance that carries electricity and heat well.
Electricity: A stream of electrons or other charged particles moving through a substance.
Insulator: A substance that does not transfer an electric current or heat.

and become stable. Put sodium and chlorine in a container together, and sodium will lose its electron and become a cation (Na⁺). Chlorine takes the same electron and becomes an anion (Cl⁻). The Na⁺ bonds with the Cl⁻ to form NaCl, sodium chloride, or the salt we use in food.

All ionic compounds are formed by cations and anions bonding. This gives each ionic formula unit a positively charged part and a negatively charged part. Each part of the formula unit is attracted to another part with the opposite charge in a different formula unit. As a result, ionic compounds tend to connect in regular patterns called crystals. Because each formula unit is held firmly in place by all the other formula units around it, ionic crystals tend to be hard solids that do not bend or break easily. Because of the strength of the attraction between ions, it takes a lot of energy to pull them apart. Heating the solid provides enough energy to pull some of the ions apart, so they melt into a liquid. The temperature at which a substance melts is called its melting point. Further heating separates the ions more until the liquid boils to produce a gas. The temperature at which this happens is called the boiling point. Ionic compounds tend to have high melting and boiling points.

When an ionic compound is dissolved in water, the ions separate and float freely in the water. These floating ions can carry electricity through the water. The ability to conduct electricity when dissolved or melted is another common property of ionic compounds.

CHARTING ELECTRONS

Chemists show how atoms form bonds by drawing atoms in a simple way. The nucleus is a central circle and is surrounded by layers of electrons. During chemical reactions electrons move between atoms or are shared in the outer shells of two atoms. The diagram below shows how an electron moves from a sodium atom to a chlorine atom to make sodium and chloride ions. The ions bond together to make sodium chloride, or common salt.

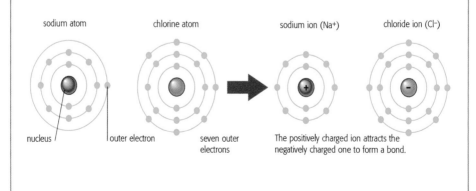

sodium atom   chlorine atom   sodium ion (Na+)   chloride ion (Cl−)

nucleus /   outer electron   seven outer electrons

The positively charged ion attracts the negatively charged one to form a bond.

COVALENT BOND

water molecule (H₂O)

hydrogen atom (H)

oxygen atom (O)

hydrogen atom (H)

shared electron

Atoms share pairs of electrons to form a stable molecule.

Water is a covalent compound.
Two hydrogen atoms share electrons with one oxygen atom.

What Is a Covalent Bond?

A covalent bond is formed when two nonmetal atoms share their electrons to become stable. Instead of one electron moving into the outer shell of another atom, the shells overlap to share the electron. Each electron becomes bonded to both the nuclei.

A group of atoms held together with bonds like this is called a covalent molecule. Hydrogen atoms form the simplest covalent molecules. Hydrogen has only a single electron and only needs two electrons to become stable instead of eight. A hydrogen atom shares its electron with another hydrogen atom, forming an H_2 molecule. Hydrogen is found in nature as H_2.

Six other elements form molecules in a similar way: oxygen (O_2), nitrogen (N_2), fluorine (F_2), chlorine Cl$_2$), bromine (Br_2), and iodine (I_2).

Sand (silicon dioxide) and water are two of the most common compounds on the surface of Earth. Both are covalent compounds. However, silicon dioxide forms hard crystals, while water is a liquid.

CREATING RUST

Place an iron nail in a jar. Cover the nail completely with water and add two tablespoons of salt. Put the lid on the jar. Come back and check the nail in about an hour. What do you see? You are watching a chemical reaction in action:

iron + oxygen → iron oxide

A new ionic bond between iron and oxygen forms to create iron oxide, or rust. Salt and water help the reaction go faster. The rust should look like dark, reddish spots on the nail.

→ When it gets wet, iron reacts with oxygen to form rust: a red, flaky iron oxide.

Because all covalent bonds involve the sharing of electrons, covalent compounds tend to have similar properties. The crystals of covalent compounds fall into two types. The first type is similar to an ionic crystal because all the atoms are connected to each other by a strong bond. This is the case with diamond, which is an extremely hard form of pure carbon. Diamond is the hardest substance known. Silicon dioxide, which is the scientific name for sand and quartz, also forms hard crystals in this way. Both diamond and silicon dioxide have high melting and boiling points because of the strong network of bonds inside their crystals. The other type of covalent compounds do not form crystals in the same way. They have no strong forces to bond molecules to each other. Instead only weak forces, called van der Waals forces, pull molecules together. Because these forces are so weak, solids are only formed at very cold temperatures. In normal conditions, the covalent compounds are gases or liquids. For example, carbon dioxide is normally a gas and will only form a crystal at very low temperatures.

Because electrons are shared in covalent compounds, there are no free-floating charged

↑ Copper (left) and zinc (center) are metal elements. They can be mixed together to form an alloy called brass (right). Inside the alloy, the copper and zinc atoms are joined by metallic bonds.

particles to conduct electricity. As a result, covalent compounds tend to be good insulators. Covalent compounds that include carbon (C) and hydrogen (H) are called organic compounds. Many burn easily when exposed to oxygen and are used as fuels. Gasoline, for example, is a mixture of several organic compounds. The term organic is used for these compounds because many were originally made by living organisms.

Metallic Bonds

Metals are generally hard solids. They tend to be flexible, too. The atoms are held together by metallic bonds, and a metal's properties are a result of these bonds. Metallic bonds

Metallic bonds make it possible for metals such as copper (shown here) to be pulled into long, thin wires. This is called being ductile. Metals are also malleable—they can be flattened into thin, flexible sheets that bend but do not break easily.

occur when metal atoms share a pool of electrons. Unlike a covalent bond, where electrons are shared but still bound to a nucleus, electrons in a metallic bond are free to move around.

KEY TERMS

Covalent bond: A bond in which two or more atoms share electrons.

Ionic bond: A bond produced when oppositely charged ions are attracted to each other.

Metallic bond: A bond between a group of metal atoms that are sharing a pool of electrons.

Van der Waals force: A very weak bond that attracts molecules to each other.

PENNY EXPERIMENT

Sand the edge of a penny so the outer layer of copper is rubbed away, exposing zinc underneath. Place the penny in 0.125 gallon (0.5 L) of vinegar for one hour. Now remove the penny and add 1.5 ounces (50 g) of Epsom salts and 2 ounces (60 g) of sugar to the vinegar. Use alligator clips to attach electrical wires to the sanded penny and a new, clean penny. Lower the pennies into the vinegar, making sure they do not touch. Connect the clean penny to the negative terminal of a large battery. Connect the sanded penny to the positive terminal. After 10 minutes, the clean penny should have a dark, silvery coating of zinc on it. You used electricity to break the metallic bonds between copper and zinc on the sanded penny. The vinegar, salts, and sugar helped move the zinc from the positively charged penny to the negatively charged penny. Scientists call this electroplating.

↑ A new penny is bright and shiny. After a few years of regular use, it will be dark like the older pennies shown here.

← An electric current flows between the two pennies through the mixture of vinegar, salts, and sugar. The zinc is carried by this current from the sanded penny to the other coin.

A piece of solid silver consists of atoms floating in a pool of free electrons. All the metal atoms give away their single outer electron, which make up a negatively charged pool of electrons. This negative charge is attracted to the positive charge of the atoms' nuclei. This attraction bonds the metal atoms together.

Although metallic bonds make most metals hard solids, they also allow the atoms inside to move past each other. This property is what makes metals ductile and malleable. Ductile solids can be pulled into thin wires, and malleable ones are easily flattened into sheets. The pool of electrons holds the metal atoms together as the solid is reshaped and prevents the solid from breaking.

What Are Isomers?

Isomers are molecules that contain the same atoms but are arranged in different ways. They have the same chemical formula but have a different shape. Understanding isomers is important in chemical reactions because isomers have different atoms available for bonding.

ISOMER STRUCTURES

The compound C_3H_8O has three forms, or isomers. The isomers have different chemical properties. Two of them are types of alcohols, while the other is an ether.

Propan-1-ol

carbon atom

hydroxyl group (–OH)

hydrogen atom

oxygen atom

▲ This alcohol molecule is called propan-1-ol. The hydroxyl group, which all alcohols have, is attached to the first carbon (1) atom.

Propan-2-ol

hydroxyl group (–OH)

▲ This alcohol molecule is called propan-2-ol because the hydroxyl is bonded to the second carbon (2) atom.

Methyl-ethyl ether

oxygen atom

▲ The third isomer is not an alcohol. Instead the oxygen atom is bonded to two carbon atoms. Molecules like this are called ethers.

Good examples of isomers are organic compounds with the formula C_3H_8O. These molecules take three forms. Two are a type of alcohol known as propanols. Alcohols are a group of organic compounds. Alcoholic drinks contain an alcohol called ethanol. However, propanol and all other alcohols are extremely poisonous. In propanol molecules, the oxygen atom is bonded to any of the three carbon atoms and to a hydrogen atom.

Together, the hydrogen and oxygen form a hydroxyl group (−OH). All alcohols have a hydroxyl group, which plays a role in chemical reactions. The two C_3H_8O alcohols are called propan-1-ol and propan-2-ol.

In the third C_3H_8O molecule, the oxygen bonds between two carbons. This compound is not an alcohol. Instead, it is an ether called methyl-ethyl ether. Ethers react in a different way to alcohols.

CHAPTER 3

Types of Chemical Reaction

There are five basic types of chemical reaction. Scientists categorize them by how chemical bonds are formed or broken. Reactions are written down as chemical equations.

Chemical reactions occur when new bonds are formed between atoms to create new compounds. Chemists have names for many different types of chemical reactions. The type of chemical reaction depends on how the reactants change to make the products.

The five main types of chemical reactions are combination, decomposition, displacement, redox, and combustion. These are general groups, and it is possible for a chemical reaction to be a member of more than one group at the same time.

← Chemical reactions can involve reactants and products in different states. For example, reacting liquids can produce gases.

Some elements are involved in nuclear reactions. These are different than chemical reactions. Instead of rearranging the bonds, a nuclear reaction changes the atom by changing its nucleus, not by rearranging its electrons. In the process it changes one element into an entirely new one.

Combination Reactions

A combination reaction occurs when two or more reactants combine to form one product: A + B → AB. In more complex cases where there are several reactants, more than one product can be formed by this type of reaction. Common compounds, such as

---

ROBERT BOYLE

Robert Boyle (1627–1691) was one of the first chemists. His work helped future scientists figure out what was happening during chemical reactions. Boyle was born in Ireland but lived in England. He became interested in chemicals as he looked for a way of turning common metals into gold. He failed but learned several things in the process.

In 1661, Boyle published *The Skeptical Chemist*, in which he suggested that matter was made of many elements. Before this, people thought earth, air, water, and fire were elements that made up everything. Boyle also showed how gases changed as they were heated and squeezed. A hot gas takes up more room than a cold gas, and when a gas is squeezed, it gets hotter. This relationship is called Boyle's law. The law helped later chemists understand what gases are made of.

← Robert Boyle and Denis Papin are shown here in Boyle's laboratory in London, England. The laboratory contains furnaces and flasks used to heat reactants and collect the products.

COMBINATION REACTION

carbon
C

oxygen
O_2

carbon dioxide
CO_2

↑ The diagram above shows a combination reaction between carbon (C) and oxygen (O_2). These reactants combine to form carbon dioxide gas (CO_2).

water, carbon dioxide, and salt, are all the products of combination reactions.

When carbon burns, it is taking part in a simple combination reaction. Oxygen combines with carbon, producing carbon dioxide gas. The chemical equation representing this is:

$$C + O_2 \rightarrow CO_2$$

↑ This is the reaction when charcoal burns. Charcoal is mainly carbon.

This is also an example of a combustion reaction and a redox reaction.

Decomposition Reactions

A decomposition reaction is the opposite of a combination reaction. It occurs when a single compound breaks down into two or more simpler substances:

$$AB \rightarrow A + B$$

When you open a can of soda, carbon dioxide bubbles are formed by a decomposition reaction. The soda contains carbonic acid (H_2CO_3) dissolved in water. This mixture is squeezed inside a soda can under high pressure. When the can is opened, the pressure inside drops. This causes the acid to decompose and form water and bubbles of carbon dioxide gas that give the soda its fizz. The decomposition reaction looks like this:

$$H_2CO_3 \rightarrow H_2O + CO_2$$

KEY POINTS

All chemical reactions obey the law of conservation of mass, which says that matter cannot be made or destroyed. During a chemical reaction, the bonds are rearranged, but the total number of atoms of each element always stays the same. The number of atoms on each side of a chemical equation will always be identical.

Displacement Reactions

A displacement reaction occurs when a more reactive atom replaces a less active atom in a compound. A reactive atom is one that forms bonds easily. Chemists divide displacement reactions into two types: single and double displacements.

A single displacement reaction occurs when the reactive atom doing the replacing is an element: $A + BC \rightarrow AB + C$. A double displacement occurs when the atom doing the replacing is already combined in another compound: $AB + CD \rightarrow AD + CB$.

Double displacement reactions often happen in solutions. A solution is a mixture in which a solid is spread out evenly in a liquid until it has disappeared. This process is known as dissolving. Seawater is a solution of salt.

Double displacements are either precipitation reactions or neutralization reactions. In a precipitation reaction, one product is a compound that cannot dissolve. Instead it forms a precipitate, or a solid that is separate from the solution. Precipitates eventually sink to the bottom of the solution.

In a neutralization, one of the products is always water. The compounds that undergo neutralization reactions are called acids and bases. Acids are compounds that contain hydrogen ions (H^+). Bases contain negative hydroxide ions (OH^-). When acids and bases react, they form water and another

DECOMPOSITION REACTION

carbonic acid
H_2CO_3

water
H_2O

carbon dioxide
CO_2

↑ Shown here is the decomposition of carbonic acid into water and carbon dioxide.

DISPLACEMENT REACTION

| tin | lead chloride | tin chloride | lead |
| Sn | $PbCl_2$ | $SnCl_2$ | Pb |

⬆ The diagram above shows how tin displaces lead when added to a solution of lead chloride.

compound. This second product is neither an acid nor base and is described as a salt. The acid and the base are said to have neutralized one another. An example of a neutralization occurs when household ammonia (a base; NH_4OH) is added to vinegar (an acid; CH_3COOH). The vinegar's H^+ ions and the ammonia's OH^- ions combine to form water (H_2O). The NH_4^+ ion bonds with the ion from the vinegar ($CH_3CO_4^-$). This forms ammonium ethanoate ($H^+OH^-NH_4^+CH_3CO_2^-$).

Redox Reactions

A redox reaction occurs when electrons move from one of the reactants to the other. Combination, combustion, and single displacement reactions are also considered redox reactions. The word redox is short for "reduction-oxidation." Each redox reaction involves two separate reactions that occur at the same time. One half of the reaction occurs when one compound gains electrons. Chemists say an atom that has gained electrons has been reduced. The other half

➡ This picture shows a displacement reaction in progress. The silver-colored strip of zinc dissolves in the blue copper sulfate solution. Red-brown copper metal forms at the bottom of the test tube.

KEY TERMS

Dissolve: To form a solution.
Insoluble: A substance that cannot dissolve.
Precipitate: An insoluble solid formed by a double displacement reaction between two dissolved compounds.
Solute: The substance that dissolves in a solvent.
Solution: A mixture that contains a dissolved substance. Solids usually dissolve in liquids.
Solvent: The liquid that solutes dissolve in.

ACID OR BASE?

Chemists use a substance called an indicator to test if something is an acid or a base. The indicator changes color when acid or bases are added to it. You can make an indicator at home from red cabbage.

Chop up a whole red cabbage into small pieces. Boil the pieces for 30 minutes. (Ask an adult to help you, and be careful with the hot water.) The boiling cabbage will make the water turn red. Let the water cool and then use a sieve to separate the cabbage from the water.

Put the red water in two cups. Add a teaspoon of baking soda to one of the cups. Baking soda is a base. Add a teaspoon of vinegar to the other cup. Vinegar is an acid. What colors do you see? Try testing other substances to see if they are acids or bases.

↑ Boiling red cabbage makes a substance called anthocyanin that mixes with the water. The color of the anthocyanin depends on how many hydrogen ions are also in the mixture. Acids have many hydrogen ions, while bases do not have any.

acid solution

base solution

hydrogen ion

hydroxide ion

acid   base

↑ Red cabbage indicator turns red when an acid is added and purple with a base.

↑ The color of an indicator depends on how many hydrogen ions (H^+) are present. Chemists measure the amount of H^+ in a solution as its pH. This stands for "potential hydrogen." A solution with a low pH has a lot of hydrogen ions in it. Acids have a low pH. Bases have a high pH. Instead of H^+ ions, they have a large number of hydroxide ions (OH^-). When OH^- and H^+ ions meet, they combine into water (H_2O). Water is neutral—it is not an acid or a base. It has a pH of 7. Anything with a pH below 7 is an acid. Bases have a pH of more than 7.

↑ Zinc reacts with an acid. The products of this reaction are a zinc compound and pure hydrogen gas. The gas bubbles out of the liquid. This is both a displacement and a redox reaction. The zinc has displaced the hydrogen from the acid. It has also lost electrons and been oxidized. The acid has gained electrons and been reduced.

of this reaction, which happens at the same time, occurs when another compound loses electrons. Chemists say an atom that has lost electrons has been oxidized.

The burning of hydrogen is a redox reaction. The two halves of the reactions are written with the following equations:

$$2H_2 \rightarrow 4H^+ + 4 \text{ electrons}$$
$$O_2 + 4 \text{ electrons} \rightarrow 2O^{2-}$$

The two halves are combined into:

$$2H_2 + O_2 \rightarrow 2H_2O$$

The hydrogens have given their electrons to the oxygens and have been oxidized. The oxygens have gained electrons from the hydrogens and have been reduced.

Combustion Reactions

A combustion reaction occurs when a compound reacts with the oxygen in the

HYDROGEN AND OXYGEN

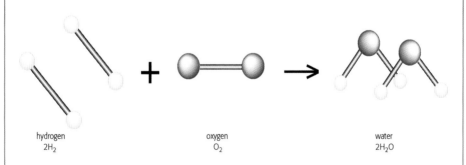

hydrogen
$2H_2$

oxygen
O_2

water
$2H_2O$

↑ This diagram shows a very simple redox reaction: hydrogen burning with oxygen to form water. The hydrogen is oxidized while the oxygen is reduced.

REDOX REACTIONS

Redox reactions are everywhere in nature, and they are used a lot by people, too, especially to purify elements.

Photosynthesis and respiration are both redox reactions. Another takes place when you slice open an apple. Once exposed to the air, the inside of the fruit turns brown in a short time. This happens because substances in the fruit are oxidized by oxygen in the air. They then form a brown compound called melanin.

Redox reactions are also used to purify some metals. Metals are found in nature as part of compounds called ores. A redox reaction is used to remove the metal atoms from the ore. The most common reaction of this type is smelting. Smelting is used mainly to purify iron. During smelting, iron ore is heated with carbon. The carbon reacts with the ore and forms a compound with the atoms that were previously bonded to the iron. This leaves pure iron behind. The iron ore has been reduced while the carbon has been oxidized.

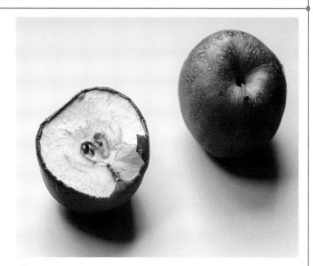

↑ Apples turn brown due to redox reactions.

↑ Molten (liquid) iron is poured into a cast after being purified in a smelter. The smelter uses a redox reaction between carbon and iron ore.

CREATING PHOTOSYNTHESIS

Photosynthesis is a redox reaction that occurs inside plants. You can watch it happen in a simple activity. Place a small piece of pondweed in a glass jar full of water. Cover the jar with a saucer and, holding them together, turn them upside down. Quickly fill the saucer with water to stop water from leaking out of the jar. A small amount of air should be trapped in the jar. Mark the level of the water with a pen and put the jar in a sunny place.

Soon there will be bubbles on the plant, and the water level may have dropped slightly. The plant is using sunlight to react water with carbon dioxide to make oxygen and sugar. The sugar is the plant's food.

← Photosynthesis produces bubbles of oxygen, which increase the amount of gas in the jar.

air and burns, producing flames and heat. Combustion reactions are often used by people to release heat.

Compounds known as hydrocarbons are often burned in combustion reactions. The name hydrocarbon is used because the compounds are made from carbon (C) and hydrogen (H). For example, propane gas (C_3H_8) is burned in cooking stoves to produce heat for cooking food. The reaction looks like this:

$$C_3H_8 + 5O_2 \rightarrow 3CO_2 + 4H_2O$$

Hydrocarbon fuels are extracted from petroleum oil and natural gas. They

COMBUSTION REACTION

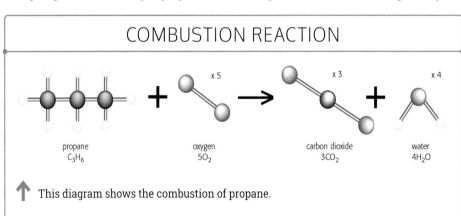

| propane C_3H_8 | oxygen $5O_2$ | carbon dioxide $3CO_2$ | water $4H_2O$ |

↑ This diagram shows the combustion of propane.

are often called fossil fuels because they are the remains of plants and other living things that were buried millions of years ago.

Writing Chemical Equations

Chemists write chemical equations to describe what happens during a chemical reaction. Chemical equations can be written simply, with only the most necessary information included. However, they can also be written in great detail, giving much more information about what happens and what is needed for a reaction to happen.

A simple example of a chemical equation is when two hydrogen atoms combine: $H + H \rightarrow H_2$. This equation shows that two hydrogen atoms (H) combine into

a hydrogen molecule (H_2).

A more detailed chemical equation might include other symbols, letters, and numbers. Much of the extra information added by these symbols is obvious to chemists or is not vital, so such symbols are not always included in equations. However, the symbols can add useful information about how to perform the reaction successfully. An arrow pointing up indicates that a product will form a gas

A mixture of propane and butane gas explodes in a ball of fire. Explosions are combustion reactions that occur very quickly and release large amounts of heat and gas all at once.

KEY TERMS

Detailed chemical equations may include the following symbols:

Symbol	Meaning
Δ	Energy (usually heat) is needed to start the reaction.
$\uparrow$	Gas will bubble out of the solution.
$\downarrow$	A precipitate will form in the solution.
$\leftrightarrow$	The reaction easily goes in both directions.
(s)	The compound is a solid.
(l)	The compound is a liquid.
(g)	The compound is a gas.
(aq)	The compound is aqueous, or dissolved in water.

that will bubble out of the solution. Carbon dioxide gas is a product of several decomposition reactions and is indicated like this: $CO_2\uparrow$. An arrow pointing down indicates that a product will form as a precipitate and sink to the bottom of a liquid. Metals, including silver (Ag), often precipitate in displacement reactions and are indicated like this: $Ag\downarrow$.

A two-headed arrow between the reactants and the products indicates that the reaction can go in both directions easily. This means that the reactants form the products and the products can also form the reactants. Instead of writing two equations ($A + B \rightarrow AB$ and $AB \rightarrow A + B$), chemists combine the two: $A + B \leftrightarrow AB$.

In a detailed chemical equation, letters in parentheses are used to indicate the state of matter of each compound. A solid is indicated with (s), a liquid is indicated with (l), and a gas is indicated with (g). When a chemical is dissolved in water, it is described as aqueous (from *aqua*, the Latin for "water") and is indicated with (aq).

Sometimes it is easy to predict the states of matter involved in an equation, but not

A BALANCE

When a reaction occurs in both directions at the same speed, a dynamic equilibrium is produced. In this system, reactants are combining to form a product, but at the same time, the product is splitting up to form the reactants again. These two processes happen at the same speed, so although reactions are always taking place, the amounts of reactants and products stays the same. Hydrogen (H_2) and iodine (I_2) react to form hydrogen iodide (HI) in a dynamic equilibrium. The reaction is represented with the equation:

$$H_2 + I_2 \leftrightarrow 2HI$$

← A chemist uses a method called titration to measure how much of a reactant is present in a mixture. A second reactant is poured into the first using a measuring tube called a burette.

always. Water is usually in liquid form: $H_2O(l)$. However, water involved in reactions with a lot of heat often turns into a gas: $H_2O(g)$. While symbols and states of matter are often helpful pieces of a chemical equation, the numbers are the most important to chemists.

Looking at the Numbers

A balanced equation shows how much of the reactants are needed to produce a certain amount of the products. Chemists alter the amount of a reactant added to a reaction to predict how much of a product will be created. In a chemical equation, there are two types of numbers, but only one of these can be changed by the chemist.

The small number to the lower right of an element indicates how many atoms are needed. For example, the "2" in H_2O shows that there are two hydrogen atoms in a molecule of water. There is also one oxygen atom, but the "1" is never written. If you do not see a number, you can assume there is only one atom. Chemists can never change the small numbers in a compound in order to balance an equation because that would imply different bonds between the atoms.

The larger number to the left of a compound is called a coefficient. The coefficient tells you how many of those molecules are needed. For example, $3H_2O$ means there are three water molecules taking part in the reaction. You can multiply the coefficient by the number of atoms in each molecule to count the total number of atoms. In this case, there are six hydrogen atoms (3×2) and three oxygen atoms (3×1).

KEY TERMS

Chemical equation: Symbols and numbers that show how reactants change into products during a reaction.
Chemical formula: A combination of chemical symbols that shows the type and number of elements in a molecule. H_2O is the formula for water, which contains two hydrogen (H) atoms and one oxygen (O).
Chemical symbol: Letters used to represent a certain element, such as O for oxygen or Na for sodium.
Coefficient: A number placed in front of a chemical formula to show how many molecules are used or produced by a reaction. $3H_2O$ stands for three water molecules.

BALANCING TIPS

If you get stuck balancing a complicated chemical equation, try putting a coefficient of 2 in front of the most complicated compound in the reaction. Then work to make the other atoms match. If this does not work, try again with a coefficient of 3. Keep increasing this coefficient until you find the balance.

Balancing the Equation

Chemists balance equations by changing the coefficients so that the number of atoms in the reactants equals the number in the products. For example, the equation for making hydrogen molecules $H + H \rightarrow H_2$ is balanced because the number of atoms is the same on both sides. However, the equation for reacting hydrogen with oxygen to make water is more complex. Both hydrogen and oxygen exist as molecules of two atoms: H_2 and O_2. Water contains atoms of both elements, but the simple equation $H_2 + O_2 \rightarrow H_2O$ does not balance. There is one oxygen atom in the product, but two oxygen atoms used as the reactants. To balance this equation, you would add a coefficient to the reactants to match the number of atoms in the products: $2H_2 + O_2 \rightarrow 2H_2O$. Now the number of atoms is the same in the reactants and the products, so the equation is balanced.

Using a Table to Balance

The chemical reaction to make water is fairly simple, so balancing the equation is easy. When equations get more complicated, it can be helpful to draw a table to help you balance numbers in the reactants and products. The table lists the number of atoms of each element.

Here is a table for $2H_2 + O_2 \rightarrow 2H_2O$:

	Reactants	Products
H	2 × 2 = 4	2 × 2 = 4
O	1 × 2 = 2	2 × 1 = 2

It is clear that you have a balanced equation because there are four atoms of hydrogen and two atoms of oxygen in both the reactants and the products.

When you balance an equation, you add or change coefficients until the numbers of atoms on both sides of the table match.

Take a look at this equation of the reaction between phosphorus (P_4) and oxygen (O_2): $P_4 + O_2 \rightarrow P_2O_5$. This equation has an unbalanced number of atoms:

	Reactants	Products
P	4	2
O	2	5

To begin balancing the equation, look at the most complicated compound (P_2O_5) and add a coefficient of 2. This will give you four phosphorus atoms and ten oxygen atoms in the products. Now balance the reactants. Oxygen molecules (O_2) each have two atoms in them, so five molecules would be needed to have ten atoms. Add a coefficient of 5 to the oxygen reactants. There are already four phosphorus atoms in the reactants, so you have finished. Using these numbers, the balanced equation would be:

$$P_4 + 5O_2 \rightarrow 2P_2O_5$$

The number of atoms is the same in the reactants and products, so the equation is balanced.

Reality

With a balanced equation, a chemist knows how many reactants are needed to create the products. However, in reality, they cannot count the number of atoms easily in a laboratory. Instead, chemists calculate the number of atoms in a substance by weighing it.

Atoms are counted in moles. The word "mole" represents a number, just as a pair equals two, a dozen is equal to 12, and a gross is 144. A mole is equal to 602,213,670,000,000,000,000,000 (6.022×10^{23}). This number represents the number of atoms or molecules in a set weight of a compound. The number is called Avogadro's number. It is named for Italian scientist Amedeo Avogadro (1776–1856), who discovered that a set amount of any gas always contains the same number of atoms or molecules. On the periodic table, an element's atomic mass number is equal to the number of grams a mole of that element weighs. For example, helium has an atomic mass of 4. This means that one mole of helium weighs 4 grams (0.14 ounces).

Compounds have molecular (covalent) or formula unit (ionic) masses. That is the sum of all the atomic masses of the atoms inside a molecule or formula unit. For example, the molecular mass of sodium chloride is roughly 58.5—23 for sodium and 35.5 for chlorine. Therefore, a single mole of sodium chloride weighs 58.5 grams (2 ounces).

Chemists use these weights to measure exactly how much of an element or a compound has been used up or produced in a chemical reaction. In reality, that is the best way to figure out how the atoms have recombined to form compounds.

Giant balloons float down Broadway in New York City as part of a Thanksgiving parade. The balloons float because they contain helium gas. Helium atoms are smaller and lighter than the atoms in the air. A mole of helium contains the same number of atoms as a mole of other elements but weighs much less.

CHAPTER 4

Energy in Chemical Reactions

Almost every chemical reaction involves an energy change. Energy is absorbed or released in a chemical reaction, and all reactions need a boost of energy to start the process.

Chemical reactions involve the two basic components of the universe— matter and energy. So far, you have seen how matter is involved in chemistry. Now it is time for the energy part.

Energy is the ability to do work. Work is done when matter is moved by a force. Lifting weights is work, as is bending metal or breaking stones. Energy comes in many forms. Electricity, light, heat, and movement

⬆ Energy is always being converted from one form to another. Water falls over a cliff and gains motion energy, while lightning converts electrical energy into light energy.

CALORIES

A calorie is a unit of energy. The word calorie with a lowercase c is the amount of energy needed to heat one gram (0.35 ounces) of water by 1 degree Celsius (1°C; 1.8°F). The word Calorie with a capital C is used to describe the amount of energy contained in food. One food Calorie is actually equal to 1,000 standard calories. That means a 300-Calorie candy bar contains 300,000 standard calories.

are all types of energy. Most chemical reactions involve adding and releasing heat energy. The study of heat is called thermodynamics. The study of heat energy during chemical reactions is known as thermochemistry.

Movement and Energy

At the level of individual atoms, there are two main forms of energy involved in chemical reactions: kinetic and potential energy. Kinetic is the energy contained by things that move. When you throw a ball, you give it kinetic energy. When you boil a pot of water, you increase the kinetic energy of the water molecules. As the molecules move faster, they break free of each other and become gas. In the same way, when you heat the reactants in a chemical reaction, you increase their kinetic energy and make the reaction proceed more quickly.

Chemists study the kinetic energy of atoms and molecules because it can affect whether or not a chemical reaction will take place. Particles with a lot of kinetic energy move rapidly and are more likely to bump into each other. If the right particles hit one another hard enough, they react with each other and break and make chemical bonds.

Potential Energy

Potential energy is stored energy. A skier at the top of a slope has potential energy. Once the skier begins to ski downhill and move faster and faster, the potential energy is converted into kinetic energy. A battery also has potential energy in chemical form. When the battery is connected to an electric circuit, the potential energy is converted to electric energy.

A bond between two atoms also contains potential energy. When the bond is broken during a chemical reaction, this potential energy fuels the reaction and is used to form the bonds of the products. Any energy left over by the reaction is then released as heat.

For example, when we eat, our bodies extract useful chemicals, such as sugars, that contain a lot of potential energy. The substances are stored, but when they are needed, they are reacted with oxygen in the blood to release their energy.

When you are running or taking exercise in other ways, you need to breathe in plenty of oxygen in order to release the energy that moves your body. That is why you breathe much faster at these times than when you are resting.

JULIUS ROBERT VON MAYER

Julius Robert von Mayer was a doctor. He was the first person to realize that living creatures use redox reactions to release energy from food. Von Mayer was born in Heilbronn, Germany, in 1814. After becoming a doctor, he took a job as a ship's doctor on a voyage to Jakarta, Indonesia. On the long voyage, von Mayer made many observations about heat and temperature. For example, he noticed that in rough seas, the water was warmer than when it was calm.

In his role as doctor, he noticed that when sailors were injured in warm climates, their blood was brighter red than it was when the weather was cold. Blood carries oxygen from the lungs to the rest of the body, and its color becomes lighter as it picks up more oxygen. Mayer realized that people required less energy to heat their bodies in hotter parts of the world. Their bodies therefore consumed less oxygen, which remained in the blood.

A Slinky moves from one level to another. As it is pushed off the top level, the spring's potential energy is converted into kinetic energy and the spring moves to the level below.

Temperature

The kinetic energy of a group of molecules involved in a chemical reaction is measured as temperature. Temperature is a measure of how fast, on average, the molecules are moving inside a substance. Objects with many fast-moving particles have a high temperature. As the particles slow down, the object becomes cooler.

GAS MOLECULES

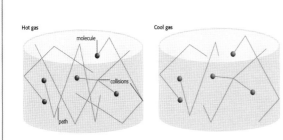

Hot gas

molecule

collisions

path

Cool gas

⬅ Gas molecules are always moving. When they are hot, gas molecules have more kinetic energy and move more quickly. They hit each other and the sides of a container harder and more often than cold gas molecules.

Heat and temperature are often thought of as being the same thing, but chemists see them as two different concepts. When molecules collide with other objects, such as your skin on a hot day, they transfer some of their kinetic energy to the object. That transfer of energy is called heat. On a hot day, you are colliding with many moving air molecules and absorbing a lot of their energy. It is this increase in heat that makes you feel warm.

Changes in Energy

Energy must be added to break a chemical bond. Just as a boulder at the top of a hill will only begin to roll after being given a push, a chemical bond will not

CONSERVING ENERGY

Energy cannot be made from nothing or turned into nothing. So, when scientists talk about energy being required or produced during a reaction, they are really talking about energy changing from one form into another. This is the law of conservation of energy, which says that energy cannot be made or destroyed.

For example, a light bulb converts electrical energy into light and heat energy, and when you rub sandpaper on wood, it gets hot as the movement energy is converted into heat. Chemical reactions convert energy as well. Burning fuel converts the energy inside chemical bonds into heat.

⬆ A Newton's cradle shows how the kinetic energy of a moving ball is transferred to a stationary one. One ball stops moving, and the next begins to move.

MEASURING STORED ENERGY

To measure the energy stored in a substance, such as fuel or food, chemists use a calorimeter. A sample is sealed in a container and lowered into water. Electricity burns the sample, warming the surrounding water. The rise in the water's temperature is then used to calculate the energy released by the burning sample. Energy is measured in units named joules. One joule (1 J) is the energy used to move 1 kg (2.2 pounds) through 1 m (3.2 feet) in 1 second.

break and release its potential energy without first being given a similar push by added energy. After a chemical reaction has ended, there is almost always a difference between the energy added to the reactants and the energy released by the products. This difference is called the enthalpy. The enthalpy of a reaction depends on the compounds involved and the strength of the bonds that are being broken or built.

In the chemical reaction $AB \rightarrow A + B$, energy is required to break the AB bond. The energy used to break the bond is added by heating molecules of AB. Once AB breaks into A and B, the bond's potential energy is released as heat. However, breaking the bond releases less heat than the amount needed to break it in the first place. Chemists call this an endothermic reaction because it absorbs heat. Endo means "inside" and thermic means "heat."

Cold packs used to reduce the swelling in injuries use endothermic reactions. Cold packs are full of reactants kept separate by a barrier. Snapping the pack breaks the barrier so the reactants mix and begin an endothermic reaction.

The reaction absorbs heat from the surroundings. This has the effect of making anything touching the cold pack, such as a swollen ankle, colder. The chemical reaction $A + B \rightarrow AB$ also releases energy when the

⬅ A person swings glowsticks to make patterns of light. The glowsticks work by using an exothermic reaction. The reaction releases energy as light rather than heat.

AB bond is built. This extra energy is given off as heat. Chemists call this an exothermic reaction. The term exo means "outside." Heat packs that warm skiers' hands use exothermic reactions. When you snap a heat pack, you break a barrier, allowing the reactants to mix and begin an exothermic reaction. Heat is given off, warming things near the heat pack. Heat energy always flows from hot objects to colder ones, so the heat pack's heat is transferred to its surroundings.

Heat packs do not make enough heat to burn, but some exothermic reactions get much hotter. Combustion reactions are a type of exothermic reaction that produce so much heat, flames and explosions are produced.

Energy Diagrams

Chemists write chemical equations to show what happens to matter during a reaction. In a similar way, they produce energy diagrams to show what happens to energy during a reaction (see p. 46). An energy diagram is a graph that shows the amount of energy contained by the molecules of reactants as they collide and react, as well as how much energy is contained in the molecules of product at the end of the reaction.

The horizontal axis of the graph represents time. The farthest left is the start of the chemical reaction, and the farthest right is the finish. As you move from left to right, time moves forward. At first the reactant

➡ Potassium reacts with water. This reaction is highly exothermic, releasing heat and light in a flash of purple flame.

> ## KEY TERMS
>
> **Endothermic reaction:** A reaction that absorbs heat energy.
> **Enthalpy:** The change in energy during a chemical reaction.
> **Exothermic reaction:** A reaction that releases heat energy.
> **Heat:** The transfer of energy between atoms. Adding heat makes atoms move more quickly.
> **Temperature:** A measure of how fast molecules are moving.

➡ A burning fuse is used to set off explosives. Explosives are chemicals that release huge amounts of energy when they react. The fuse supplies the energy the explosives need to begin reacting.

molecules come together and collide. They then react and form the products. Finally, these separate into individual molecules.

The vertical axis represents energy. As you go up this axis, energy increases. The bottom of the graph is low energy and the top is high energy. The line that is drawn on the diagram shows the amount of energy at each stage before, during, and after the reaction.

Energy diagrams often look like a hill. The energy starts low, increases and reaches a peak, then goes down again. The top of the "hill" represents the activation energy. That is the amount of energy it takes to make a reaction happen. The activation energy is the minimum amount of kinetic energy needed for the reactants to collide strongly enough for them to react and form the products.

ENERGY DIAGRAM

Energy diagrams show how different reactions use energy.

USING THE ENERGY

Cars cannot run without a fuel such as gasoline. Burning gasoline provides the energy needed for the car to move forward, but how does that happen? The engine converts the gasoline's potential energy into movement in several steps. **1)** Gasoline mixed with air is pumped into a cylinder, which is fitted with a piston that can move up and down inside. **2)** The piston moves up and squeezes the fuel, making it heat up. **3)** An electric spark makes the hot fuel react with oxygen in the air and explode. The reaction produces several gases, which are very hot—the gasoline's potential energy has become heat energy. Hot gases expand quickly, and the expanding gases push on the piston, forcing it to move down. The heat energy has now been converted to movement, or kinetic energy. The up and down movement of the piston is converted by gears to the spinning motion of the car's wheels. **4)** Finally, the piston rises again and pushes out the used gases, ready to repeat the process.

The activation energy can be read from an energy diagram. It is the difference between the energy level of the reactants and the peak.

Energy diagrams also tell you whether a reaction is endothermic or exothermic. If the reactants have higher energy than the products, then overall energy has been released. The reaction is exothermic. If the products have higher energy than the reactants, then energy has been absorbed. The reaction is endothermic.

KEY TERMS

Activation energy: The minimum energy needed for reactants to change into products.
Energy: The ability to do work.
Energy diagram: Shows the change in energy levels as reactant molecules come together and change into products.
Work: A term scientists use to describe when matter is moved by adding energy.

CHAPTER 5

Measuring the Speed of Reactions

Chemists can control the speed of chemical reactions using a number of different methods. They can change how fast the molecules are moving and how tightly packed they are.

The rate of a chemical reaction is how fast the reactants turn into the products. Some reactions happen quickly, such as when gunpowder explodes in an instant. Other reactions happen slowly, like a copper statue corroding over many years. The rate of reaction depends on how the reactants come into contact with each other.

➡ Chemical reactions run at different speeds, or rates, depending on conditions. Chemists measure how quickly the products are formed from the reactants to calculate the rate.

Reactant particles must physically bump into each other in just the right place for a chemical reaction to take place. In general, small and simple reactants are more likely to hit in just the right place because there is less room for error. Large and complicated reactants have a harder time because they can contact each other in several ways.

To understand this idea better, imagine that you have two sets of shapes: a pair of squares and a pair of octagons. When a particular side of each shape touches the other, the shapes stick together. It will likely be faster to find the connecting side of the squares than the octagons. The squares have only four sides to try, while the octagons have eight.

The same thing happens in chemical reactions. Small, simple reactants form products quickly, while large, complex reactants tend to form products slowly. Larger reactants are less likely to collide with each other in the correct position for a reaction.

Starting a Reaction

Before you can measure the rate of a reaction, the reaction has to get started.

RANDOMNESS AND ENERGY

The second law of thermodynamics says that chemical reactions always increase the amount of entropy, or randomness, in a system. This idea can be confusing.

The law does not say that the entropy of all the products will be higher than that of the reactants. Some reactions decrease entropy, such as when hydrocarbon gases are used to make plastics. However, the law says that the entropy of the entire universe will always increase. Chemists think big!

← This silver cup has been tarnished with less-ordered silver compounds. Its entropy has increased. People polish their silver to keep it looking bright and shiny.

⬆ Ice melts into water. Inside the ice, the water molecules are arranged in an ordered pattern. As the ice melts, the molecules of water become less ordered and more random. Chemists say that the entropy of the water molecules has increased. If matter is left alone, its entropy tends to increase.

Some chemical reactions are spontaneous, meaning the reactions begin on their own. Other reactions need energy to be added before they can start. To understand how a spontaneous reaction works, think of two rooms connected by a closed door. One room contains air fresheners to make the room smell like flowers; the second room does not. When you open the door between the two rooms, some of the air freshener will naturally flow into the second room. Soon both rooms will smell like flowers, but the scent will not be as strong. Nothing is pushing or blowing the scent; it just spreads out. This movement is caused by what chemists call entropy.

THE RATE OF RUST

In the rust creating activity on page 20, we saw how iron and oxygen reacted to make iron oxide, or rust. You can repeat this reaction to investigate how different conditions affect the rate of reaction. You'll need three jars and three new nails. In jar 1, repeat the activity as before. Ask an adult to cover the nail in jar 2 with boiled water and put the lid on. In jar 3, place a nail with no water and put the lid on.

Return the next day to compare the results. By changing the conditions, you change the rate of the reaction. The nail in jar 1 will have rusted as before. The boiled water in jar 2 contains very little oxygen, so hardly any rust will have formed. The reaction runs more quickly in wet conditions, so little to no rust will have formed in jar 3. However, over a long time, moisture in the air may help the nail rust.

SLOWING THE GROWTH OF BACTERIA

When you put your leftover dinner in the refrigerator, you slow the chemical reactions that threaten to spoil your food. We say food is spoiled, or rotten, when unwanted bacteria grow in the food, making it taste bad. Spoiled food can also make you ill.

The bacteria use chemical reactions to grow. Putting the food in a refrigerator lowers the food's temperature, slows the rate of the reactions, and slows the growth of bacteria. This means your food takes longer to spoil, and you can eat the leftovers later.

Entropy is a measure of how random, or disordered, a system is. Most things in nature lack order, including many things in chemistry. The oxygen atoms in the air are not stacked neatly. They move randomly. Disordered systems have high entropy. How much entropy something has depends on its state of matter and on the surrounding conditions. With a lot of atoms or molecules moving around, a gas has high entropy. With many atoms packed in place, a solid has much less entropy. The entropy of a liquid is somewhere in between.

In a chemical reaction, the entropy of the reactants partly determines how the reaction begins and how fast it goes. A spontaneous reaction is driven by entropy. Just as the air freshener moves from one room to another, reactants move together and form products in a spontaneous reaction.

Reactions that are not spontaneous require something to get started. Usually, energy is added to the system to make the reactant molecules move fast enough so that they can react when they collide.

How fast a chemical reaction forms products depends on how often and how hard the reactants bump into each other. There are two things that determine the number of collisions between reactants: concentration and temperature.

Concentration of Chemicals

Imagine octagons with sticky sides. If only two octagons are moving around randomly in a room, like gas particles, it may take those octagons a long time to bump into each other in such a large space. However, if you increase the concentration— i.e. the number of octagons in the same space—you will have better luck. A thousand octagons in the same room will be much closer together and therefore hit each other far more often. Because there are more collisions between octagons, pairs will form more quickly.

In most cases, the concentration of reactants affects how fast the reaction will occur because it determines how likely reactants are to bump into each other in the right way. If the concentration of reactants is high, the reaction will be fast. If the concentration of reactants is low, the reaction will be slow.

↑ The colder food is, the slower chemical reactions inside it take place. In frozen foods, they stop almost completely. Frozen food can be kept for several weeks and still be good to eat.

If a reaction involves several reactants and takes place in a series of steps, this general rule about the effect of concentration may no longer be true. The reaction can only proceed as quickly as its slowest stage. Therefore it is the concentration of just the reactants involved in that stage that determines the rate. Increasing the concentrations of the other reactants will have no effect.

Heat and Reactants

Just as the concentration of the reactants affects the chance of colliding in the right spot, so does the temperature. Remember that temperature is a measure of how fast atoms or molecules move. Cold temperatures show that molecules are moving slowly. High temperatures occur when molecules move quickly. Cold, slow-moving molecules are less likely to collide and begin the

THE SIZE AND SPEED OF A REACTION

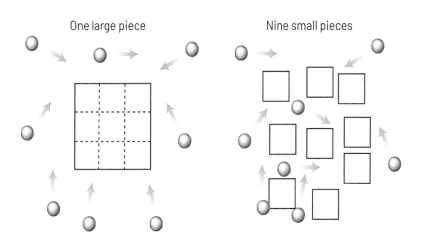

One large piece   Nine small pieces

⬆ This diagram shows how the same amount of solid will come into contact with other reactants more quickly when broken into pieces.

⬅ Calcium carbonate reacts with acid, producing carbon dioxide gas. The beaker on the left contains powder, while the one on the right contains a single piece of the carbonate. Carbon dioxide is being produced more quickly in the left beaker, making it fizz.

When one of the reactants is a solid, the size of its pieces will affect the speed of the reaction. The reaction takes place on the surface of the solid, where the reactants come into contact. A large solid has a small surface area compared with its weight. Most of the reactant is locked away inside the solid and cannot take part in the reaction. Therefore the reaction is slow. If the solid is crushed into a fine powder, its total surface area is hugely increased. More of the reactants can take part in the reaction, which now takes place much more quickly.

↑ Copper oxide is heated with zinc in a test tube. The reaction produces pure copper and zinc oxide. The reaction occurs more quickly when the mixture of reactants is heated.

chemical reaction. That is why food that is kept cold will not react with the air and spoil. Hot, fast-moving atoms are more likely to collide in the right way and react. This is also why food cooks faster at higher temperatures but burns at a certain point. However, that is not the whole story. The energy that atoms possess at different temperatures also affects reaction rates. At low temperatures, atoms often do not have enough energy to form bonds, even if they do collide in the right place. At high temperatures, atoms are not only more likely to collide, they are also more likely to have enough energy to get the reaction going when they do.

Controlling a Reaction

Concentration and temperature are two things that affect the rate of a reaction. These factors can be altered during a reaction, and they play a part in all reactions. Chemists can also introduce substances to slow or speed up the rate of reaction. A catalyst is something that speeds up reactions. An inhibitor is something that slows or stops reactions. These are neither reactants nor products, and they are unchanged by the chemical reaction taking place. Catalysts and inhibitors work by changing the activation energy—the amount of energy the reactants need to begin the reaction. However, they do not change how much energy is released or absorbed by a reaction.

Catalysts decrease the activation energy, so more of the reactants form products at low temperatures. Catalysts often work by providing a surface where reactants come together and react without requiring a lot of energy. For example, the catalytic converters in cars use a thin layer of platinum and iridium as catalysts. These metals help remove the harmful gases produced by burning gasoline and diesel fuel. The harmful gas molecules cling to the surface of the catalysts, where they can react with oxygen and become less dangerous gases. For example, the converter changes carbon monoxide gas (CO), a poison, into carbon dioxide (CO_2).

Inhibitors increase the activation energy. As a result, fewer of the molecules collide with sufficient energy to form products, and the reaction slows down. Inhibitors often work by bonding with the reactants, so other molecules cannot make contact. Many reactions that take place inside living cells are controlled by inhibitors.

CHAPTER 6

Electrochemistry

Some chemical reactions generate electricity. Electrochemistry uses these chemical reactions to produce electric currents that can be converted into light energy and mechanical energy.

Electrochemistry uses redox reactions to produce electricity. A redox reaction happens when electrons move from one compound to another. In electrochemistry, the electrons that are exchanged during redox reactions are forced to travel from one place to another. These traveling, charged particles create an electric current.

Redox is short for reduction-oxidation, the two halves of the reaction. The reduction occurs when one compound gains electrons. The oxidation occurs when one compound loses electrons. Chemists use something called a voltaic cell to harness the electricity produced by the reactions. The voltaic cell is named for Alessandro Volta (1745–1827), an Italian scientist who invented the device in 1799. The volt (V), the unit used for measuring the strength of an electric current, is also named for him.

← Batteries contain chemicals that produce electric currents when they react.

Voltaic Cells

A voltaic cell is a pump that forces electrons to move from one place to another. In a simple voltaic cell, two dishes of chemical solutions are connected by a U-shaped pipeline. One dish is where the reduction reaction takes place; the other dish is where the oxidation reaction takes place. The electrons must travel between the two dishes through a wire. The pipeline is filled with a solution of ions to carry the electrons.

Each dish also contains a stick of metal called an electrode. Metals are good conductors of electricity because they have many free-floating electrons inside. The metal electrodes serve as a holding tank of electrons, ready to carry a current when needed, once they are connected to each other with a wire.

The electrode where the reduction reaction takes place is called the cathode. The cathode is usually labeled with a " − " because the current of electrons flows away from it. The oxidation-reaction electrode is called the anode. The anode is labeled with a " + " because the current flows toward it.

The electrodes are immersed in a liquid that contains the reactants for the redox reaction. The two halves of the reaction happen continuously until one of the reactants runs out. In the reduction reaction, a reactant gains electrons from the anode to become the product. This product then joins onto the anode, gradually building up a thin layer. In this way, the anode is constantly supplying the reactants with electrons. At the cathode, the opposite

MICHAEL FARADAY

English chemist Michael Faraday (1791–1867) is remembered for investigating electrochemistry. The son of a blacksmith, Faraday taught himself chemistry by reading books and by helping out in laboratories as a boy. As an adult, he established the laws of electrolysis and the link between electricity and magnetism. He made the first electric motor and generator and coined the terms electrolyte, electrode, anode, and cathode.

⬆ Shown here are Michael Faraday (left) and John Daniell, another English chemist, in Faraday's laboratory. Daniell is known for inventing a type of battery.

happens. The reactant is being oxidized and is giving away electrons. The cathode collects these electrons. The electrons flow through the wire between the electrodes. Electrons are negatively charged, so they flow away from the negative cathode to the positive anode. The current contains energy, and this energy can be transported along wires to provide power to run machines.

Voltaic cells can use many different types of chemicals in the redox reactions, but they often contain metals. One reaction involves zinc and manganese dioxide. The pure zinc is oxidized into zinc hydroxide and releases electrons. The manganese dioxide is reduced by gaining electrons.

Batteries

A battery is a portable voltaic cell. Batteries come in many shapes, sizes, and powers, but they all work by storing chemical energy and turning it into electrical energy using a redox reaction.

All batteries contain an anode (the flat, negative end) and a cathode (the raised, positive end). Instead of a U-shaped tube, the electrodes are separated by a mixture of chemicals called electrolytes.

Electrolytes contain ions. Ions are formed when atoms gain or lose electrons. This gives the atoms a charge. Positive ions have lost electrons, while negative ions have gained them. The ions flow through the electrolyte and carry the charge between the electrodes.

When a battery is sitting on a table, the redox reaction is not happening inside because there is nothing connecting the anode and cathode. When you put your battery into a device, such as a flashlight, you create a path between the anode and

AMMETERS

scale
needle
spring
magnet
coil
Ammeter

An ammeter (left) measures the size of an electric current. It contains a coil of wire that is surrounded by a magnet. When an electric current passes through it, the coil produces a magnetic force that pushes against the magnet. This force makes the coil twist around and move a needle. The needle moves along a scale that shows how large the current is. When the current is switched off, the coil and needle are pulled back into the starting position again by a spring. Electric current is measured in amperes (A). One ampere is a current where 6.25 million trillion electrons pass through a circuit every second.

EXPERIMENT WITH A LEMON

You can make a voltaic cell with a citrus fruit. Press a lemon on the table and roll it to release the juice inside. Push a 2-inch-long (5 cm) copper wire into the side of the lemon. This is the cathode. Push a straightened paper clip into the lemon next to the copper. This is the anode. They should both be 1 inch (2.5 cm) deep and must not touch.

Touch your tongue to the cathode and anode at the same time. What do you feel? A reaction in the cell releases electrons that move through your tongue. You should feel a slight tingling in your tongue, but it will not hurt!

cathode. That completes a circuit and the redox reaction begins. The circuit is a circular path through which electricity can flow. If there is a break in the circuit, the electricity will not flow.

When the redox reaction begins inside the battery, electricity is produced. A fixed amount of reactants is stored in the battery. When the reactants are completely used up, we say the battery is "dead." A dead battery can no longer produce electricity because the chemical reaction is not taking place.

Some batteries are rechargeable. They work the same way as a regular battery, but when a rechargeable battery becomes dead, you plug it into an electrical outlet. Electricity from the outlet forces all the reactions inside a rechargeable battery

DANIELL CELL

The Daniell cell is a type of voltaic cell invented by John Daniell (1790–1845). The anode is solid copper and the cathode is zinc metal. The cell has two electrolytes. The anode is in a copper sulfate solution, while the cathode is in sulfuric acid. The two liquids are separated by a porous barrier. The zinc atoms in the cathode are oxidized. They lose two electrons and form zinc ions (Zn^{2+}). These ions dissolve in the acid. The copper ions (Cu^{2+}) in the copper sulfate are reduced. They pick up electrons from the anode and form copper atoms, which join onto the anode.

↑ The electrons released in the cathode move through a wire to the anode, producing an electric current of 1 volt.

KEY TERMS

Anode: Where oxidation reactions occur in a voltaic cell.

Cathode: Where reduction reactions occur in a voltaic cell.

Electrode: A storage tank for electrons in a voltaic cell.

Electrolyte: Liquid containing ions that carries a current between electrodes.

Voltage: The force that pushes electrons through an electric circuit

INSIDE A BATTERY

Modern batteries are more complex than voltaic cells, but they use electrochemical reactions in the same way. Here, below, the cathode is a paste containing manganese dioxide. This paste is also the electrolyte. The anode is powdered zinc. A metal rod transfers electrons from the cathode to the rest of the circuit.

to run in reverse. The anode becomes the cathode, the cathode becomes the anode, and the products of the reaction become the reactants. This generates a new source of the original reactants so the battery can make electricity again.

Electrolytic Cells

Electrolytic cells are the opposite of voltaic cells. Voltaic cells use a redox reaction to produce electricity. Electrolytic cells use electricity to produce a redox reaction. Electrolysis is the process of pushing electricity through a solution to force a reaction to occur. The reaction generally involves a stable compound being broken apart by electricity. During the electrolysis of water, for example, water molecules are broken into their hydrogen and oxygen atoms. Chemists run electricity through liquid water to start the reaction, which has the basic equation:

$$2H_2O \rightarrow 2H_2 + O_2$$

Like all redox reactions, the electrolysis of water has two halves. The water is reduced at the cathode. The molecules receive electrons. This causes them to split into hydrogen gas (H_2) and hydroxide ions (OH^-):

$$2H_2O + 2 \text{ electrons} \rightarrow H_2 + 2OH^-$$

MAKING AN ELECTRIC BATTERY

Electric batteries were once called piles because they were made from stacks, or piles, of voltaic cells. You can make your own pile using a stack of pennies and dimes, a paper towel, and some concentrated lemon juice. The coins are the electrodes, the penny is the anode, and the dime is the cathode. Lemon juice is the electrolyte.

Use a strong paper towel so it does not break apart when it is wet. Cut the paper towel into ten 1-inch (2.5 cm) squares. Soak them in the lemon juice. Clip one end of an electric wire to a penny, and begin building a stack in this order: penny, dime, paper towel, penny, dime, paper towel, and so on. Use all the paper towel pieces and end with a dime on top. Connect a second wire to this top dime. Connect the loose ends of the wires to an ammeter. Switch the wires if you do not get a reading.

You can repeat the experiment using salty water instead of lemon juice. The piles could also be made with aluminum foil and iron nails. These will give a slightly different size of electric current.

↑ This electric battery is made from pennies and dimes. A pair of coins on top of each other makes a single cell. The paper towel is used to divide one cell from another. The juice can pass through the paper, so an electric current will run through the whole pile. Connect an inexpensive ammeter or voltmeter to see how much current is produced.

← Water is split into hydrogen and oxygen gas using electrolysis. Gas bubbles form on electrodes and are collected in upside-down test tubes. Twice as much hydrogen (left tube) is produced as oxygen.

Fuel Cells

A hydrogen fuel cell uses hydrogen and oxygen gas to make electricity. A hydrogen fuel cell is like a battery, but it has a different source of reactants. A battery has reactants stored inside. Space is limited, and when the reactants run out, the battery dies. The reactants for a fuel cell are stored outside and pumped into the cell, so space is not a problem. In a hydrogen fuel cell, hydrogen and oxygen are combined to form water. As they react, the energy released is used to produce electricity. Hydrogen fuel cells are an attractive source of power because they do not produce any harmful pollution, just water vapor.

In the electrolysis of water, the ions stay in the water, but the hydrogen forms gas bubbles on the electrode that float up out of the water.

At the anode, the water is oxidized. The electrons are released by the water molecules to make oxygen atoms and hydrogen ions (H^+):

$$2H_2O \rightarrow O_2 + 4H^+ + 4 \text{ electrons}$$

The oxygen bubbles out of the liquid like the hydrogen. The electrons travel along a wire to the cathode and take part in the reduction of more water molecules.

Using Electrolysis

Electrolysis is used to separate pure metals from their compounds. That is called electrorefining. The process used is the same as the one to break water apart. In nature, most metals are found as compounds.

Electrolysis is often the only way to extract reactive metals. The metal compounds are dissolved or melted to make an electrolyte. Electrolysis provides the energy needed to remove the metal atoms from the compound. The atoms collect at one electrode. Waste material forms at the other.

The same electrolysis process is used to coat objects with a thin layer of metal. This is called electroplating. When you buy an inexpensive gold necklace, it is likely to be another type of metal covered with a very thin layer of gold.

During the electroplating process, the object to be coated becomes the cathode. The valuable metal used for the coating is the anode and is also dissolved in the electrolyte. Electrolysis deposits the anode metal onto the cathode.

⬆ Inexpensive items of jewelry are coated with a very thin layer of precious metal by electroplating. This necklace is gold-plated.

BATTERIES AT HOME

⬆ This 9-volt battery is made up of six cells piled on top of each other. Each cell is 1.5 volts.

The batteries that you put in flashlights, radios, remote controls, and other portable electronic devices contain several voltaic cells stacked on top of each other. The stacked cells, called a pile, can generate more electricity than a single cell. The size of the battery indicates something about the number of cells inside. A 9-volt battery has six 1.5-volt cells in a pile. A 12-volt car battery has six 2-volt cells in a pile.

CHAPTER 7

Nuclear Reactions

In the mid-20th century, scientists discovered nuclear reactions. These turn one element into another element, and the process releases enormous amounts of energy. Nuclear power is used in medicine, agriculture, and industry, as well as for destructive purposes.

Nuclear reactions are reactions that involve the particles inside the nucleus of an atom. All chemical reactions involve the electrons in the space surrounding the nucleus. Nuclear reactions are different because they change one element into another by changing the number of protons in the nucleus of the atom.

⬆ The sun's heat and light are produced by nuclear reactions at its center.

Instability

Nuclear reactions involve a set of elements that chemists describe as radioactive. Radioactive elements have unstable atoms. The nuclei of these atoms often break apart, especially when they collide with another particle, such as a neutron. Elements with 83 or more protons in the nucleus are the most radioactive.

The instability is a result of there being so many protons packed into the nucleus. Protons are positively charged, so they are constantly pushing against each other. The reason they do not fly apart from each other is a stronger force that holds the protons and neutrons together. This force, called the strong nuclear force, only works over tiny distances. It has no effect outside the nucleus. In the nucleus of an unstable atom, the strong force is not powerful enough to keep all the particles together. Eventually the nucleus begins to break apart, or decay.

Radioactive decay occurs when the nucleus gives off small particles. These particles are also often called radiation. There are three types of radiation, each named after Greek letters: alpha, beta, and gamma. An alpha particle is two protons and two neutrons, a beta particle is a single electron, and a gamma ray is an emission of energy.

WHAT IS NUCLEAR POWER?

Nuclear power plants use the energy released by nuclear reactions to generate electricity. The heat from the reactions is used to boil water and make steam. The steam is used to spin large fans called a turbine. The turbine's spinning motion is converted into electricity by a generator. Coal and gas power plants do the same thing, but they use coal or oil fires to heat the water.

water tank

Steam is piped to a turbine.

Heat from reactor boils water.

generator

turbine

Nuclear reactions take place inside the reactor.

← This diagram shows how the heat from nuclear reactions is used to make electricity.

↑ Power plant workers wear suits, gloves, and hoods to protect themselves from radiation leakage from a nuclear reactor. They breathe through masks that filter out the radioactive particles from the air.

Radiation

If you have already heard of nuclear reactions, it is probably because of the health concerns over radiation. High doses of radiation damage living cells so they die or cause dangerous illnesses.

Nuclear radiation burns the skin in the same way sunlight causes sunburn. Inside the body, radiation is more dangerous. It breaks up the contents of cells so they no longer work properly. The radiation may damage the cell's DNA, which causes the

→ This picture shows the path of alpha particles being released by a speck of radium. The radiation is released equally in all directions.

↑ Melted glass containing radioactive waste from a nuclear reactor is poured into a mold. The glass prevents radiation from leaking out. This technique is being investigated to see if glass is a safe way to store the dangerous radioactive waste produced by nuclear reactors.

cell to work in the wrong way. DNA stands for deoxyribonucleic acid, which is the molecule that contains the information needed to organize a living cell. Damaged DNA causes illnesses. For example, the cell might begin to grow too quickly and become a cancerous tumor.

Radiation spills are a huge concern when building nuclear power plants. If something goes wrong in a nuclear power plant, radiation can be released into the air and harm living things in the area. For example, in 1986, an explosion at a reactor in Chernobyl, Ukraine, spread radiation over the homes of 200,000 people. Everyone had to be evacuated.

Another major concern with nuclear power plants is the radioactive waste they produce. Nuclear reactions continue in this radioactive waste and can emit dangerous amounts of radiation for 10,000 years or more. The waste must be stored for all that

GEIGER COUNTERS

A Geiger counter is used to measure all types of radiation. Inside the Geiger counter is a tube filled with gas. When radiation enters the tube, it knocks electrons off the gas molecules, turning them into ions. The electrons are picked up by a wire running inside the tube and produce a pulse of electricity. Each pulse shows that one particle of radiation has collided with the gas in the tube.

radiation particle

wire

gas tube

electron

gas ion

loudspeaker

scale

power supply

↑ This diagram shows how a Geiger counter works. The counter shows how much radiation is in the tube on a scale and by producing clicks.

time. Despite the concerns over safety and the costs of storing waste, nuclear power is popular because it produces less air pollution than other power sources, such as coal.

Isotopes

Certain forms of the elements are more radioactive than others. The different forms of atoms are called isotopes.

The number of protons in an atom determines what element it is. However, some atoms of the same element have different numbers of neutrons. This makes them different isotopes. Some isotopes are more radioactive than others because the number of neutrons

↑ Physicist Guy Savard examines a gas catcher cell that is part of a centrifuge that generates intense beams of nuclear isotopes.

makes them unstable.

To learn more about isotopes, it helps to understand how they are written. Chemists write isotopes in two ways.

One way to write an isotope looks like this: $_z^a X$, where "X" is the chemical symbol, "z" is the atomic number (the number of protons in the nucleus), and "a" is the atomic mass number (the sum of the protons and neutrons in the nucleus). If you subtract the atomic number from the mass number, you get the number of neutrons in that isotope. This level of detail can be useful, but it is not always needed. Chemists may just write the symbol and the mass number, such as U-238

(uranium-238, or $_{92}^{238} U$).

When some isotopes start to decay, they often cannot stop. U-238 is an unstable isotope of uranium. When it begins to decay, it produces thorium-234 (Th-234), another unstable isotope. Th-234, in turn, decays to protactinium-234 (Pa-234), another unstable isotope. The decay continues creating unstable isotopes until, after 14 unstable isotope steps, a stable atom is formed and the decay stops. Such a series of steps is known as a radioactive decay series and is not unusual among the most unstable elements.

Fission Reactions

One type of nuclear reaction is called a

KEY POINTS

Radioactive isotopes decay at specific rates. The amount of time it takes for half the isotopes in a sample to break down is called the half-life. Each isotope has a characteristic half-life, which is the same no matter what the sample size is.

CHAIN REACTION

This diagram shows how nuclear fission can cause a chain reaction. A neutron hits a uranium-235 (U-235) nucleus. The nucleus splits in two and releases two or three neutrons. The neutrons then hit more U-235 atoms and cause yet more fission reactions.

neutron

U-235 nudeus

nucleus divides

smaller nucleus

U-235 fissioning

Neutron hits another U-235.

neutrons

fission reaction. A fission reaction occurs when a neutron strikes a large nucleus, breaking it into two or more new elements with smaller nuclei. In general, the equation for a fission reaction looks like this:

$$^a_z W + n \rightarrow ^a_z X + ^a_z Y + n$$

Element W is bombarded by a neutron (n) to produce two new elements, X and Y, plus more neutrons. The letters "a" and "z" represent the atomic mass and the atomic number.

Unlike a chemical reaction, which creates bonds between different elements, a fission reaction actually creates new elements. Fission reactions also release a lot of heat and several neutrons. These neutrons are then free to bombard other radioactive nuclei and start more fission reactions. That is a chain reaction. The nuclear reactors at power plants control the chain reaction so that the heat and radiation are released slowly and safely.

Fusion Reactions

A fusion reaction is the opposite of a fission reaction. A fusion reaction combines two small nuclei to create a single large nucleus and release a lot of energy. Fusion reactions are very hard to start because they take huge amounts of energy to begin.

One place where fusion reactions happen continuously is inside the sun. The sun turns hydrogen atoms into helium by fusion and releases the energy that lights and warms our planet. On Earth, scientists have experimented with ways to generate power from fusion reactions. Because the reactions require so much energy to get started, they are not easy to investigate. Fusion reactors are being built to test whether it is possible to release more energy from a fusion reaction than is added to start it. If this is achieved, fusion could be a useful new source of power.

Nuclear Energy

The two fundamental components of the universe, matter and energy, interact during a chemical reaction. In a nuclear reaction, both matter and energy are still present and necessary, but the rules are different. Matter can be changed from one element to another during a nuclear reaction. However, matter can also be changed into energy.

A huge amount of energy is released by a nuclear reaction because some of the matter in the original nucleus is converted into energy. Because chemists know the amount of mass involved, they can calculate the energy using the famous equation, $E = mc^2$. E is energy, m is mass, and c is the speed of light. This equation was figured out by the

SUN FUSION REACTION

This diagram shows the fusion reaction that takes place in the sun. Two radioactive hydrogen isotopes— deuterium and tritium—fuse to make a single helium atom. Normal hydrogen atoms (H) have a single proton as a nucleus. Deuterium (H-2) has one proton and one neutron in the nucleus, while tritium (H-3) has one proton and two neutrons.

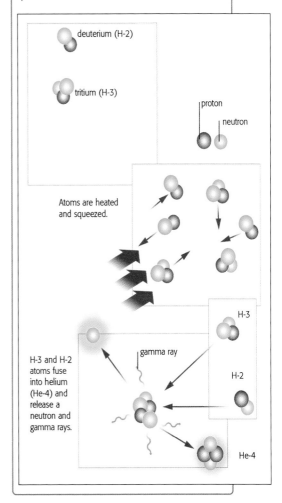

deuterium (H-2)

tritium (H-3)

proton

neutron

Atoms are heated and squeezed.

H-3

gamma ray

H-3 and H-2 atoms fuse into helium (He-4) and release a neutron and gamma rays.

H-2

He-4

great German-born American scientist Albert Einstein (1879–1955). The speed of light, it turns out, is a huge number, and as a result, small amounts of mass produce huge amounts of energy.

To balance a chemical equation, you count atoms. To balance a nuclear equation, you count the number of subatomic particles. The sum of all the atomic particles' numbers on the left-hand side must equal the sum

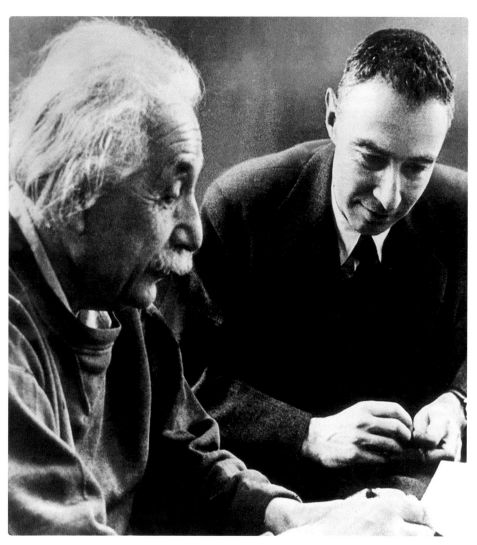

↑ Albert Einstein (left) is shown here in discussion with U.S. physicist Robert Oppenheimer. Oppenheimer was the head of the Manhattan Project, which built the first nuclear bomb. The project used Einstein's theories about matter and energy to make the bomb.

ATOMIC BOMBS

The first atomic bomb was dropped by the United States on Japan in 1945. It contained two blocks of uranium metal that were kept separate. The bomb was set off by a normal explosive, which shot the smaller metal block onto the larger one. Together, the blocks made a critical mass—a lump of uranium large enough for fission reactions to start. An uncontrolled chain reaction of fissions released heat and radiation in a huge blast. The bomb killed 140,000 people. Some people died in the explosion, but many more died afterward from the effects of radiation.

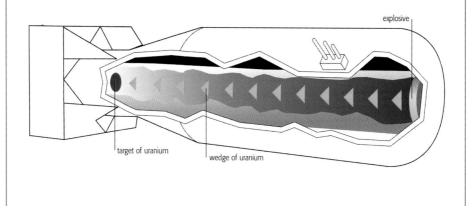

explosive

target of uranium

wedge of uranium

KEY TERMS

Atomic number: The number of protons in the nucleus.
Fission: When a large atom breaks up into two small atoms.
Fusion: When small atoms fuse to make a single larger atom.
Isotope: Atoms of the same element with different numbers of neutrons. Many isotopes are radioactive.
Radioactive decay: When small particles break off from an unstable nucleus.

of all particles on the right-hand side. None of the elements bond to make compounds; instead, one element is changed into another element.

For example, when a uranium-235 (U-235) atom is hit by a neutron (n), a fission reaction occurs. U-235 breaks into two smaller elements, barium (Ba-142) and krypton (Kr-91):

$$\ce{^{235}_{92}U + ^{1}_{0}n -> ^{142}_{56}Ba + ^{91}_{36}Kr + 3^{1}_{0}n}$$

This equation is balanced. The number of particles in the reactants (235 + 1) is equal to the products (142 + 91 + 3).

CHAPTER 8

BIOGRAPHY
Fritz Haber

Fritz Haber was a German physical chemist. His name has passed into the language of chemistry with the "Haber process," a method of manufacturing ammonia. The gas was used to make artificial fertilizers and explosives—substances that Germany was desperately short of during World War I.

Fritz Haber was born to a German-Jewish family in Breslau, Silesia in 1868. Silesia was then part of Prussia. Three years later, Prussia became the leading power in the newly formed German Empire, which was known as the Second Reich.

Haber's father was a successful merchant trading in natural dyes. He was a major importer of the natural blue dye indigo, which was obtained from plants that grew in Asia. After studying at the German universities of Berlin and Heidelberg, and at Zurich in Switzerland, Haber joined the family business as a traveling salesman.

Haber soon realized that dramatic changes were taking place in the dye industry. The future, he was sure, lay with synthetic dyes (dyes that are produced artificially through a chemical reaction). The market for the plant madder, a source of red dye, had collapsed with the development of the synthetic red dye alizarin in 1868, and

Haber knew that it would not be long before someone manufactured a synthetic replacement for indigo.

Because of disagreements with his father, Haber left the company and got a junior post in the Department of Chemical and Fuel Technology at the Karlsruhe Technical University in southwest Germany. Haber's work at Karlsruhe had two dramatically different effects. On the one hand, it saved the world from starvation. On the other, it created a way of killing and disabling many thousands of people quickly and efficiently.

Food and Weapons

In his book *Chemistry in its Applications to Agriculture and Physiology* (1840), another German chemist, Justus von Liebig, (1803–1873), concluded that among the "foods" needed by plants for healthy growth were nitrogen and potassium. He mistakenly thought that plants could get nitrogen from the air. In fact, plants absorb their nutrients from the soil. When land is intensively farmed year after year, plant yields become lower and lower unless nutrients are returned to the soil through fertilizers.

Traditional methods of farming used animal manure as a fertilizer, but the world's population was rapidly growing at the end of the 19th century. There was demand for an ever-increasing food supply. More and more land was coming into production, so huge amounts of fertilizer were needed. The question was, where could they be found?

For a time, the vast deposits of Chile saltpeter (sodium nitrate) found in the Atacama region of northern Chile provided the answer. By 1913, Chile was responsible for 90 percent of the world's supply of nitrogen-based fertilizers, with Germany taking about one-third of the annual production. However, these deposits were running out. At the start of the 20th century, scientists had begun to forecast doom, warning that a chemical solution must be found if people were to be properly fed.

The problem was particularly serious in Germany. In the years leading up to World War I (1914–1918), the country was concentrating its economic resources on building its military capabilities and becoming a leading world power. Nitrates (nitrogen-containing salts) were not only essential ingredients in fertilizers, they were also a vital component in many explosives. German leaders soon realized that, in the event of a major war, German ports would

KEY DATES	
1868	December 8, born in Breslau, Prussia
1901	Marries Clara Immerwahr, the first woman to gain a PhD in science at Breslau University
1908	Appointed professor of chemistry at Karlsruhe Technical University
1911	Becomes director of the Kaiser Wilhelm Institute for Chemistry, Berlin
1916	Appointed director of the chemical warfare service
1918	Awarded the Nobel Prize in Chemistry
1933	Is forced to leave Germany
1934	January 29, dies in Basel, Switzerland

be blockaded to cut off fresh supplies of nitrates. With no extensive nitrate supplies of its own, Germany would be unable to grow sufficient crops to feed its people properly or to supply its army with enough explosive ammunition to fight its enemies.

Nitrates could be recovered from ammonia, which is a compound of nitrogen and hydrogen. Supplies of ammonia could be obtained from coal, but only 5 pounds (2.27 kg) of ammonia could be taken from about 1 metric tonne (1.1 ton) of coal, making it very expensive. It was obvious that other sources would have to be found.

⬆ Berthold Schwarz was a legendary alchemist in the late 14th century.
He was also known as "Berthold the Black," a nickname he presumably earned
from carrying out his explosive chemical experiments.

THE ORIGINS OF GUNPOWDER

The first significant explosive, gunpowder, was known in China from about the 9th century AD and in the West from the 13th century. The English philosopher and scientist Roger Bacon (c. 1214–1292) wrote down a coded recipe for gunpowder, which, translated into modern terms, indicates that he used a mixture of charcoal (carbon), sulfur, and saltpeter (potassium nitrate). The earliest illustration of gunpowder being used in Europe dates from 1327. It shows a strange arrow-shaped missile being fired from a cannon.

The development of gunpowder led to major changes in warfare. Stone castles were no longer safe against the powerful guns of a besieging army. Even the mighty walls of Constantinople were defenseless against the cannons of the Turkish army in 1453. From the 15th century, a number of so-called "gunpowder empires" developed as European powers, backed up by cannons carried on their ships, seized territory in Asia, Africa, and America.

Key Ingredient

The nitrate saltpeter was the key ingredient in making gunpowder. At first, nitrates were extracted from decomposing animal and vegetable matter—mainly urine and manure. The supply of nitrates was so important that in most European countries, it was controlled by the state, and saltpeter workers were given key privileges. In 1625 in England, the law allowed saltpeter workers to enter any property and remove any material likely to contain nitrates. In France after 1540, saltpeter workers could claim free lodgings and transport. However, supplies remained low, and the lack of saltpeter for making gunpowder was one of the factors that brought an end to the Seven Years' War in Europe in 1763.

A more convenient and abundant supply was discovered at the start of the 19th century. Vast beds of sodium nitrate were found in northern Chile by a local woodcutter. He had built a fire and found that the ground below it started to melt. He reported the strange event to the authorities, who realized what it must be. Mining started in the region in about 1825. Over a century later, when the industry was well in decline, Chile was still producing more than 1 million tons a year. Once Haber discovered how to manufacture nitrates artificially, however, there was no longer a problem of supply.

Making Ammonia

What was needed was a way of making ammonia artificially—in other words, synthesizing it from nitrogen in the atmosphere and hydrogen extracted from coal gas. Earlier attempts to make nitrogen react with hydrogen using an electric spark failed when it was found that a temperature of up to $5,432°F$ ($3,000°C$) was needed.

When chemists find it difficult to produce a desired chemical reaction, they often resort to the use of catalysts. A catalyst

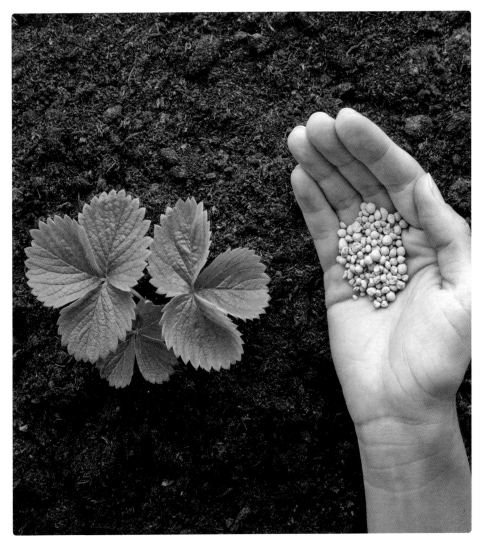

⬆ Experts warn that nitrate fertilizer, which is used to help crops grow, leaches into the groundwater and can cause water pollution up to 80 years after it is initially used.

is a substance that, when present in small quantities, can speed up a chemical reaction. The catalyst itself is not used up during the reaction. For example, poisonous carbon monoxide and oxygen will hardly react at all at room temperature, but with the aid of a sprinkling of platinum powder as a catalyst, the gases readily combine to form carbon dioxide. This is what happens in the catalytic converter that is a part in many vehicles.

Haber therefore tried to combine nitrogen and hydrogen by finding a suitable catalyst.

Nitrates were essential for making explosives during World Wars I and II.

At first he thought that the rare metal osmium was the ideal catalyst, and he acquired exclusive rights to purchase the world's entire stock of 220 pounds (100 kg). However, after testing 4,000 other catalysts, he found that specially treated iron, much more abundant and therefore cheaper, worked just as well. Consequently, in 1903, Haber succeeded in combining nitrogen and hydrogen at a temperature of 1,832°F (1,000°C) using an iron catalyst. The yields, however, were too small to be commercially useful. A colleague, Walther Nernst (1864–1941), pointed out that increasing the pressure might help the reaction. After further calculation, Haber worked out how much extra pressure would be needed to get a productive reaction.

By 1909, Haber had established that he could produce large quantities of ammonia with an iron catalyst at a temperature of 932°F (500°C) and a pressure of about 200 atmospheres. An atmosphere is a unit of pressure equivalent to 14.72 pounds per square inch (101,325 newtons per sq. m). Commercial production of ammonia by the "Haber process" began in 1913, the

HABER-BOSCH PROCESS

liquefied air (nitrogen, N_2)

gas passes over iron catalyst at a temperature of 932°F (500°C) and a pressure of atmospheres and emerges as ammonia gas ($2NH_3$)

coal gas (hydrogen, $3H_2$)

ammonia gas is cooled to -28F° (-33.43C°)

liquid ammonia

Nitrogen from liquefied air is reacted with hydrogen from coal gas at very high temperatures and pressure. The result is ammonia gas, which is condensed to produce liquid ammonia.

year before World War I started. By the end of the war, in 1918, 220,462 tons (200,000 tonnes) of synthetic ammonia were being produced annually. Thanks to Haber, Germany had remained virtually self-sufficient in its supply of this vital chemical throughout the years of the conflict.

Weapons of War

In 1911, Haber became director of the Kaiser Wilhelm Institute for Physical Chemistry in Berlin. This was an important scientific center, and on the outbreak of World War I in August 1914, Haber put his laboratory at the disposal of the German government.

He became a key figure in the development of poison gas as a weapon on the battlefield.

In 1918, Haber was awarded the Nobel Prize in Chemistry "for the synthesis of ammonia from its elements, nitrogen and hydrogen." The process that Haber had invented had produced the weapons responsible for the death and disablement of thousands of people in the war, so it seemed to many observers that this was an extremely odd award to make at this time. Many French and British scientists felt that the role Haber had personally played in developing German chemical warfare should have made him unfit to receive such an award. The British scientific journal *Nature* commented that, in introducing chlorine gas, Haber had "initiated a mode of warfare which is to the everlasting discredit of Germany."

Gold from Seawater?

Ever the patriot, Haber sought another way to serve his country. At the end of World War I, the Allies ordered Germany to pay financial reparations (a sort of fine) as a punishment. Some of this was to be paid in gold. The Allies hoped that the burden of such costs would halt any further military aggression by Germany.

Haber knew that the world's oceans contained billions of tons of gold, and he began to ponder how a chemist could recover this gold from seawater to help free Germany from its huge debts. In 1923, he and his team set up their laboratory on the liner *Hansa* and began trying to extract gold from the Atlantic Ocean as they sailed to New York. However, on this and later voyages, the amounts of gold they actually managed to recover were so tiny that Haber eventually abandoned the project in 1927.

The End of German Science

After World War I, Haber's institute in Berlin had continued to gain in importance, becoming the world's leading center of research in physical chemistry. Haber had close links with industry, and he also began building better relations with foreign scientists. In 1930, he founded the Japan Institute, which had bases in Berlin and Tokyo, to forge closer cultural and scientific links between the two countries.

In January 1933, Adolf Hitler (1889–1945) became chancellor of Germany. The Nazi Party, which he headed, blamed Jews for the country's economic and social problems and passed a series of anti-Jewish laws. In April 1933, a new Civil Service Law came into force, preventing the employment of anyone who was not of pure German descent. All university teachers and professors in Germany were employed by the state, and large numbers of them, particularly scientists and doctors, were Jewish. Hitler stated that if the loss of Jewish scientists meant the "annihilation of German science, then we shall do without science for a few years."

For Jewish scientists, leaving the country was a sensible course of action, even though the costs of doing so were high. It meant abandoning their family home, all financial assets, and perhaps a laboratory or a professional position built up over a lifetime. Non-Jewish German scientists looked on helplessly as they saw German science disappear before their eyes. Nobel Prize winners, major mathematicians, physicists, and chemists were all forced to flee the country.

Haber was Jewish. At first his leading position, famous patriotism, and previous service to the state gave him some protection. Those, like Haber, who had fought in the 1914–1918 war were exempt from the Civil Service Law. Unofficially, Haber was told that—as long as he made no fuss—his position would be secure. However, Haber would have none of this. He resigned his post and told the ministry, "For more than

⬆ On the outbreak of World War I in 1914, Haber had put his laboratory at the disposal of the German government, but his past loyalty did not count for anything under Hitler's regime due to his Jewish background. In 1933, Haber resigned his position and left Germany for the last time.

40 years I have selected my collaborators on the basis of their intelligence and their character and not on the basis of their grandmothers, and I am not willing for the rest of my life to change this method which I have found to work so well."

There was no turning back. Haber left Germany for the final time in the summer of 1933. He had already been invited to work in Cambridge, England, by Sir William Pope (1870–1939), the chemist who had been in charge of Britain's own chemical warfare program. However, Haber was to work in Cambridge for only a brief period. Soon after he moved to England, he died from a heart attack on January 29, 1934 while on vacation in Switzerland.

SCIENTIFIC BACKGROUND

POLITICAL AND CULTURAL BACKGROUND

Before 1885

French chemist Claude-Louis Berthollet (1748–1822) shows that ammonia is a compound of nitrogen and hydrogen

German chemist August Wilhelm von Hofmann (1818–1892) produces synthetic dyes known as magenta, or fuchsine, and "Hofmann's violets"

1888 Wilhelm II (1859–1941) is crowned third German emperor and ninth king of Prussia

1889 At the Hague conference, Germany and 23 other countries agree not to use chemical weapons: "projectiles whose sole object is the diffusion of asphyxiating gases"

1890

1893 Haber begins studies on decomposition of organic compounds at high temperatures

1895

1896 Haber publishes *Experimental Studies on Decomposition of Hydrocarbons*

1900 The Republican president of the United States, William McKinley (1843–1901), wins re-election on the promise of "four more years of the full dinner pail"

1902 Scottish-born author Arthur Conan Doyle (1859–1930) publishes *The Hound of the Baskervilles*, featuring his popular fictional detective, Sherlock Holmes

1900

1905 German chemist Johann von Baeyer (1835–1917) wins the Nobel Prize for chemistry for synthesizing indigo

1906 English chemist William Henry Perkin (1838–1907) is honored at a celebration dinner at the Royal Institution in London; it is the 50th anniversary of his discovery of the synthetic dye, mauve

1905

1905 Russian troops in St. Petersburg open fire on workers demonstrating in front of the Winter Palace of Tsar Nicholas II (1868–1918); more than 200 people are killed

1909 The first 3.5 ounces (100 g) of synthetic ammonia are produced by the Haber process

1910

1909 The National Negro Committee (later the National Association for the Advancement of Colored People [NAACP]) is founded in the United States

1912 German industrial chemist Friedrich Karl Rudolf Bergius (1884–1949) uses high pressure, high temperatures, and a catalyst to produce paraffins (alkanes) such as petrol and kerosene from coal dust

1913 The Haber process is developed for commercial production of nitrogen by German chemist Karl Bosch (1874–1940) of Badische Anilin- and Soda-Fabrik in Oppau, Germany

1915

1915 In April at Ypres in Belgium, German soldiers attack French and Canadian troops using chlorine gas; more than 5,000 Allied troops die

1916 In France, the Germans and French each lose 400,000 dead or wounded in the Battle of Verdun

1920

c. 1925 Commercial production of paraffins from coal dust using Bergius's process begins; it will provide important alternative fuel for Germany during World War II (1939–45)

1922 The Union of Soviet Socialist Republics (USSR) is officially established

1924 American inventor Clarence Birdseye (1886–1956), who has seen how the people of Labrador keep food fresh by freezing it, sets up the General Seafood Company selling a range of frozen foods

1925

1925 Bosch invents process for preparing hydrogen on a commercial scale

1928 In the Soviet Union, Communist leader Josef Stalin (1879–1953) tries to force peasants to work state-owned farms, or "collectives," as part of his first Five-Year Plan; those who resist are killed or sent to labor camps

1930

After 1930

1939 Swiss chemist Paul Müller (1899–1965) synthesizes dichlorodiphenyl-trichloroethane (DDT) as an insecticide

1962 *Silent Spring*, by American naturalist Rachel Carson (1907–1964), highlights the devastating effect of modern synthetic chemical pesticides such as DDT on the food chain

Periodic Table of Elements

The periodic table organizes all the chemical elements into a simple chart according to the physical and chemical properties of their atoms. The elements are arranged by atomic number from 1 to 118. The atomic number is based on the number of protons in the nucleus of the atom. The atomic mass is the combined mass of protons and neutrons in the nucleus. Each element has a chemical symbol that is an abbreviation of its name. In some cases, such as potassium, the symbol is an abbreviation of its Latin name ("K" stands for kalium). The name by which the element is commonly known is given in full underneath the symbol. The last item in the element box is the atomic mass. This is the average mass of an atom of the element.

Scientists have arranged the elements into vertical columns called groups and horizontal rows called periods. Elements in any one group have the same number of electrons in their outer shell and have similar chemical properties. Periods represent the increasing number of electrons it takes to fill the inner and outer shells and become stable. When all the spaces have been filled (Group 18 atoms have all their shells filled), the next period begins.

VIIIA	
He 2	
4.003	
Helium	

IIIA	IVA	VA	VIA	VIIA
B 5	**C** 6	**N** 7	**O** 8	**F** 9
10.81	12.01	14.01	16.00	19.00
Boron	Carbon	Nitrogen	Oxygen	Fluorine

		IIIA	IVA	VA	VIA	VIIA	VIIIA
		Al 13	**Si** 14	**P** 15	**S** 16	**Cl** 17	**Ar** 18
		26.98	28.09	30.97	32.06	35.45	39.95
		Aluminium	Silicon	Phosphorus	Sulfur	Chlorine	Argon

IB	IIB						
Cu 29	**Zn** 30	**Ga** 31	**Ge** 32	**As** 33	**Se** 34	**Br** 35	**Kr** 36
63.55	65.38	69.72	72.63	74.92	78.96	79.90	83.80
Copper	Zinc	Gallium	Germanium	Arsenic	Selenium	Bromine	Krypton
Ag 47	**Cd** 48	**In** 49	**Sn** 50	**Sb** 51	**Te** 52	**I** 53	**Xe** 54
107.9	112.4	114.8	118.71	121.76	127.6	126.9	131.3
Silver	Cadmium	Indium	Tin	Antimony	Tellurium	Iodine	Xenon
Au 79	**Hg** 80	**Tl** 81	**Pb** 82	**Bi** 83	**Po** 84	**At** 85	**Rn** 86
197.0	200.6	204.4	207.2	209	[209]	[210]	[222]
Gold	Mercury	Thallium	Lead	Bismuth	Polonium	Astatine	Radon
Rg 111	**Cn** 112	**Nh** 113	**Fl** 114	**Mc** 115	**Lv** 116	**Ts** 117	**Og** 118
280]	[285]	[286]	[289]	[289]	[293]	[294]	[294]
Roentgenium	Copernicium	Nihonium	Flerovium	Moscovium	Livermorium	Tennessine	Oganesson

- Alkali metals
- Alkali earth metals
- Noble gases
- Halogens
- Transition metals
- Lanthanoids
- Actinoids
- Metalloids
- Post transition metals
- Nonmetals

Gd 64	**Tb** 65	**Dy** 66	**Ho** 67	**Er** 68	**Tm** 69	**Yb** 70	**Lu** 71
157.3	158.9	162.5	164.9	167.3	168.9	173	175
Gadolinium	Terbium	Dysprosium	Holmium	Erbium	Thulium	Ytterbium	Lutetium
Cm 96	**Bk** 97	**Cf** 98	**Es** 99	**Fm** 100	**Md** 101	**No** 102	**Lr** 103
247]	[247]	[251]	[252]	[257]	[258]	[259]	[262]
Curium	Berkelium	Californium	Einsteinium	Fermium	Mendelevium	Nobelium	Lawrencium

Glossary

acid Substance that dissolves in water to form hydrogen ions (H^+). Acids are neutralized by alkalis and have a pH below 7.

activation energy The energy needed for reactants to change into products in a chemical reaction.

alchemist Person who attempted to change one substance into another using a combination of primitive chemistry and magic.

alkali Substance that dissolves in water to form hydroxide ions (OH^-). Alkalis have a pH greater than 7 and will react with acids to form salts.

allotrope A different form of an element in which the atoms are arranged in a different structure.

alloy A metallic substance that contains two or more metals. An alloy may also be made of a metal and a small amount of a nonmetal. Steel is an alloy of iron and carbon.

alpha particle The nucleus of a helium atom. This particle has two protons and two neutrons.

atom The smallest independent building block of matter. All substances are made of atoms.

atomic mass number The number of protons and neutrons in an atom's nucleus.

atomic number The number of protons in a nucleus.

boiling point The temperature at which a liquid turns into a gas.

bond The chemical connection between atoms.

by-product A substance that is produced when another material is made.

calorimeter Apparatus for accurately measuring heat given out or taken in.

catalyst Substance that speeds up a chemical reaction but is left unchanged at the end of the reaction.

chemical equation Symbols and numbers that show how reactants change into products during a chemical reaction.

chemical formula The letters and numbers that represent a chemical compound, such as "H_2O" for water.

chemical reaction The reaction of two or more chemicals (the reactants) to form new chemicals (the products).

chemical symbol The letters that represent a chemical, such as "Cl" for chlorine or "Na" for sodium.

combination reaction A reaction in which two or more reactants combine to form one product.

combustion The reaction that causes burning. Combustion is generally a reaction with oxygen in the air.

compound Substance made from more than one element that has undergone a chemical reaction.

compress To reduce in size or volume by squeezing or exerting pressure.

condensation The change of state from a gas to a liquid.

condensation reaction A reaction between two molecules that produces water as a by-product.

conductor A substance that carries electricity and heat well.

corrosion The slow wearing away of metals or solids by chemical attack.

covalent bond Bond in which atoms share electrons.

crystal A solid made of regular repeating patterns of atoms.

crystal lattice The arrangement of atoms in a crystalline solid.

decay chain The sequence in which a radioactive element breaks down.

decomposition reaction A reaction in which a single compound breaks down into two or more substances.

density The mass of substance in a unit of volume.

dipole attraction The attractive force between the electrically charged ends of molecules.

displacement reaction A reaction that occurs when a more reactive atom replaces a less reactive atom in a compound.

dissolve To form a solution.

ductile Describes materials that can be stretched into a thin wire. Many metals are ductile.

elastic Describes a substance that returns to its original shape after being stretched.

electricity A stream of electrons or other charged particles moving through a substance.

electrolyte Liquid containing ions that carries a current between electrodes.

electron A tiny negatively charged particle that moves around the nucleus of an atom.

electronegativity The power of an atom to attract an electron.

element A material that cannot be broken up into simpler ingredients via a chemical reaction. Elements contain only one type of atom.

endothermic reaction A reaction that absorbs heat energy.

energy The ability to do work.

energy level Electron shells represent different energy levels. Those closest to the nucleus have the lowest energy.

enthalpy The change in energy during a chemical reaction.

evaporation The change of state from a liquid to a gas when the liquid is at a temperature below its boiling point.

exothermic reaction A reaction that releases energy.

fission Process by which a large atom breaks up into two or more smaller fragments.

four elements The ancient theory that all matter consisted of only four "elements" (earth, air, fire, and water) and their combinations.

fusion When small atoms fuse to make a single larger atom.

gaseous state State in which particles are not joined and are free to move in any direction.

heat The transfer of energy between atoms. Adding heat makes atoms move more quickly.

hydrocarbon Chemical compounds that contain only hydrogen and carbon.

hydrogen bond A weak dipole attraction that always involves a hydrogen atom.

hydrolysis The process by which a molecule splits after reacting with a molecule of water.

hydroxyl A functional group (–OH) made up of an oxygen atom and a hydrogen atom.

inhibitor A substance that slows down a chemical reaction without being used up by it; also called a negative catalyst.

insoluble A substance that does not dissolve in a solvent.

insulator A substance that does not transfer an electric current or heat.

intermolecular bonds The forces that attract molecules to one another.

intramolecular bond Strong bond between atoms in a molecule.

ion An atom that has lost or gained one or more electrons.

ionic bond The attraction between positive and negative ions in an ionic compound.

ionization The formation of ions by adding or removing electrons from atoms.

isotope Atoms of a given element must have the same number of protons but can have different numbers of neutrons. These different versions of the same element are called isotopes.

liquid Substance in which particles are loosely bonded and are able to move freely around each other.

matter Anything that can be weighed.

melting point The temperature at which a solid changes into a liquid. When a liquid changes into a solid, this same temperature is also called the freezing point.

metallic bond Bond in which outer electrons are free to move in the spaces between the atoms.

mixture Matter made from different types of substances that are not physically or chemically bonded together.

mole The amount of any substance that contains the same number of atoms as in 12 grams of carbon-12 atoms. This number is 6.022×10^{23}.

molecule Two or more bonded atoms that form a substance with specific properties.

neutralization reaction A displacement reaction involving acids and bases in which one of the products is water and the other is a salt.

neutron One of the particles that make up the nucleus of an atom. Neutrons do not have any electric charge.

nucleus The central part of an atom. The nucleus contains protons and neutrons. The exception is hydrogen, in which the nucleus contains only one proton.

octet rule If an atom's outer electron shell contains exactly eight atoms (an octet), the atom will be stable and unreactive.

oxidation The addition of oxygen to a compound or the loss of electrons.

oxidation state A number used to describe how many electrons an atom can lose or gain.

oxidizer A substance that removes electrons from another substance to make its own outer shell stable.

pH A measure of the acidity or alkalinity of a substance.

photon A particle that carries a quantity of energy, such as in the form of light.

potential energy Energy that something has because of the way it is positioned or its parts are arranged.

product The new substance created by a chemical reaction.

proton A positively charged particle in an atom's nucleus.

radiation The products of radioactivity— alpha and beta particles and gamma rays.

radioactive decay The breakdown of an unstable nucleus through the loss of alpha and beta particles.

reactants The ingredients necessary for a chemical reaction.

redox reaction A reaction that occurs when electrons move from one of the reactants to the other.

reduction The addition of hydrogen to a compound or the gain of electrons.

relative atomic mass A measure of the mass of an atom compared with the mass of another atom. The values used are the same as those for atomic mass.

relative molecular mass The sum of all the atomic masses of the atoms in a molecule.

salt A compound made from positive and negative ions that forms when an alkali reacts with an acid.

shell The orbit of an electron. Each shell can contain a specific number of electrons and no more.

solid State of matter in which particles are held in a rigid arrangement.

solute A substance that dissolves in a solvent.

solution A mixture of two or more elements or compounds in a single state (solid, liquid, or gas).

solvent The liquid that dissolves a solute.

standard conditions Normal room temperature and pressure.

state The form that matter takes—either a solid, a liquid, or a gas.

subatomic particles Particles that are smaller than an atom.

temperature A measure of how fast molecules are moving.

valence electrons The electrons in the outer shell of an atom.

van der Waals forces Short-lived forces between atoms and molecules.

volatile Describes a liquid that evaporates easily.

voltage The force that pushes electrons through an electric circuit.

Further Information

American Association for the Advancement of Science
1200 New York Avenue NW
Washington, DC 20005
(202) 326-6400
Website: www.aaas.org
This international nonprofit organization is dedicated to advancing science around the world by serving as an educator, leader, spokesperson, and professional association.

American Chemical Society (ACS)
1155 Sixteenth Street NW
Washington, DC 20036
(800) 333-9591
Website: portal.acs.org
The ACS represents professionals in all fields of chemistry. Its Division of Organic Chemistry **(www. organicdivision)** specifically promotes the advancement of the field of organic chemistry.

American Institute of Chemical Engineers (AIChE)
120 Wall Street, FL 23
New York, NY 10005-4020
(800) 242-4363
Website: www.aiche.org
This is the world's leading organization for chemical engineering professionals, with more than 45,000 members from over 90 countries.

Museum of Science + Industry
5700 S. DuSable
Lake Shore Drive
Chicago, IL 60637
(773) 684-1414
Website: www.msichicago.org
One of the largest science museums in the world is home to more than 35,000 artifacts and nearly 14 acres of hands-on exhibits designed to spark scientific inquiry and creativity.

Science History Institute
315 Chestnut Street
Philadelphia, PA 19106
(215) 925-2222
Website: sciencehistory.org/visit/exhibitions
Formed by the merger of the Chemical Heritage Foundation and the Life Sciences Foundation, the Institute's museum features a permanent exhibition that explains how chemistry has influenced people, along with other changing exhibits on a variety of subjects.

Books

Berk Koch, Susan and Rauch, Micah. *Chemical Reactions!* Norwich, VT: Nomad Press, 2021.

Congdon, Lisa. *The Illustrated Encyclopedia of the Elements: The Powers, Uses, and Histories of Every Atom in the Universe.* San Francicsco, CA: Chronicle Books, 2021.

Dorling Kindersley. *The Chemistry Book.* London, UK: Dorling Kindersley, 2022.

Faust, Daniel R. *Fizz, Gurgle, and Pop! Chemical Reactions in the Lab.* New York, NY: Rosen Publishing, 2021.

Gray, Theodore and Mann, Nick. *Molecules: The Elements and the Architecture of Everything.* New York, NY: Black Dog and Leventhal, 2018.

Gray, Theodore. *Reactions: An Illustrated Exploration of Elements, Molecules and Change in the Universe.* New York, NY: Black Dog and Leventhal, 2017.

Huggins-Cooper, Lynne. *Chemistry for Curious Kids: An Illustrated Introduction to Atoms, Elements, Chemical Reactions and More!* London, UK: Arcturus, 2021.

Keyser, Amber J., and Biskup, Agnieszka. *The Dynamic World of Chemical Reactions with Max Axiom, Super Scientist.* North Mankato, MN: Capstone Press, 2019.

Linde, Barbara Martina. *Understanding Chemical Reactions.* New York, NY: Rosen Publishing 2021.

Lowe, Derek B. *The Chemistry Book: From Gunpowder to Graphene, 250 Milestones in the History of Chemistry.* New York, NY: Union Square and Co, 2022.

Moore, John T. *Chemistry Essentials for Dummies.* London, UK: For Dummies, 2019.

Morlock, Rachel. *Chemical Reactions: It Matters!* New York, NY: Rosen Publishing, 2021.

NEDU. *Chemistry Made Easy: An Illustrated Study Guide for Students To Easily Learn Chemistry.* Cheyenne, WY: NEDU LLC, 2021.

Scientific American. *Ask the Experts: Chemistry.* New York, NY: Rosen Publishing 2018.

Scientific American. *Chemistry Magic.* New York, NY: Rosen Publishing 2023.

Sezer, Ali O. *Chemistry: An Illustrated Guide for All Ages.* New York, NY: Barron's, 2021.

Smithsonian. *The Elements Book: A Visual Encyclopedia of the Periodic Table.* New York, NY: Dorling Kindersley, 2017.

Sterling Education. *High School Chemistry: Comprehensive Content for High-School Chemistry.* New York, NY: Sterling Education, 2022.

Index

Photo Credits